MILTON

53SP 33
October 2019
Brooklyn, NY

53rdstatepress.org

MILTON
© PearlDamour 2019

MILTON is made possible by the New York State Council on the Arts with the support of Governor Andrew M. Cuomo and the New York State Legislature.

Cover design: Jonathan Crimmins
Book design + layout: Tyler Crumrine

ISBN: 978-0-9978664-2-1
Library of Congress Control Number: 2019912095

Printed in the United States of America

MILTON

a performance & community engagement experiment by PearlDamour

53rd State Press
Brooklyn, New York
2019

Aug. 5, 2014: *A tiny former Episcopal church, home of the Women's Club, on a quiet street corner in Milton, North Carolina, population 250. On the street outside, a Department of Transportation sign flashes "PLAY ABOUT MILTON. WHAT DOES IT MEAN TO BE AMERICAN?" People are leaving their homes and walking to the play. Inside, chairs and church pews are arranged in a circle. Five plexiglass screens, hanging from the rafters, glow with video footage of the sky. It's a full house, with Black and white people of many ages. Towards the end of the show, Helga Davis, a Trinidadian-American actor from New York City says, "And in the cemetery, you look down and see a tire decorated with flowers on the gravestone, and you know this must be Miss Patsy's Dad's grave." Miss Patsy, sitting near her, takes Helga's hand. Both women begin to cry.*

June 10, 2016: *McLoughlin High School Auditorium, Milton-Freewater, Oregon, population 7,027. In the lobby a banner reads: "Welcome to Milton," and identifies five towns named Milton on a map of the U.S. Inside the theater, the audience sits onstage on risers that form a circle. There's an opening act: two local cowboy balladeers, Coyote Joe and Little Joe, both with guitars. It's a full house, about ¾ white, ¼ Latinx. In the middle of this bilingual version of the show, there is a five-minute audience conversation in small groups. Lisa asks, "If there was one thing you could change about the world, what would it be?" Coyote Joe pipes up: "Impeach Obama."*

May 15, 2017: The community room in the basement of the Milton Public Library in Milton, Massachusetts, population 25,575. This is a multi-purpose meeting and education room, with chairs on wooden risers in a circle. Here, the sky videos look like little oval "sky portals" projected on the walls. We are in the part of the show when actors assign beliefs to specific audience members. They've moved through controversial beliefs about family, religion, race, and immigration. Then, one of the actors points straight at an audience member and says, "You believe paying three dollars to have a bag of trash removed is RIDICULOUS." The whole room cracks up—the rising price of trash collection has been a hot topic among locals lately.

introduction

PearlDamour is the collaborative team of Katie Pearl and Lisa D'Amour.

Our performance work has grown in cities: Austin, Minneapolis, New Orleans, and New York, circulating inside a small, urban network of artists, educators, and theater enthusiasts who are interested in questions about aesthetics, ethics, and form. How can theater continue to break away from linear narrative? How is theater accountable to the communities in which it is performed? How can interdisciplinarity help us invigorate and reimagine the theatrical event? These questions have pushed us into new territory with each project.

In 2012, after about 15 years making work together, we were beginning to feel restless. It was an election year, and patriotic commercials were blaring platitudes about what it meant to be an American. We thought, well, what DOES it mean? If the U.S. flag is a symbol of our country, why does it seem to belong to conservatives and not liberals? What is our relationship to this land? How can we claim it as home?

We knew we couldn't answer these questions by staying inside our urban bubble.

So we began to imagine a show made from visiting small towns. What if we went to visit five towns of the same name, in different parts of the country, with very different geographical features, economies, political affiliations, and racial demographics? We Googled "most common city names." Milton was number 18. It spoke to us. Katie had an Uncle Milton. Perhaps we'd reference *Paradise Lost*. And from there, using a combination of practicality and instinct, we chose five of them: Louisiana, Wisconsin, Massachusetts, North Carolina, and Milton-Freewater, Oregon. We imagined a constellation:

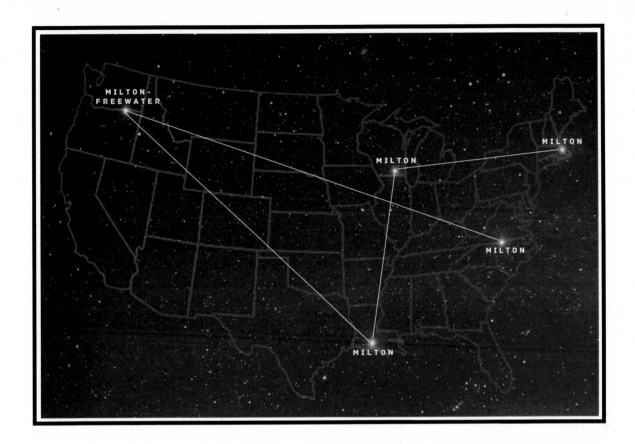

Historically, sailors looked to the stars to navigate the vast immensity of the sea. We looked to our "Milton" constellation to orient and locate ourselves within the vast concept of being American.

As we began visiting the Miltons, talking with locals, visiting churches, and getting to know civic organizations, we realized: Oh. This won't be a show just inspired by the Miltons, it will be made *for* and *with* them. We devised a working process that involved collaborating closely with each town on local arts events, adapting our performance to reflect each towns' concerns, and presenting our show for a short run in a local venue.

July 25, 2014: *It's about a week before the performance of* MILTON *in North Carolina. Hosanna Blanchard, a 25-year-old white local entrepreneur, sits at the sewing machine in the Milton Women's Club. She's sewing blackout curtains to cover the stained glass windows in this former church so we can use it as a performance space. These curtains will remain in Milton so the venue can be more easily used for future performances. Across the room, Shirley Wilson, an African American high school math teacher who sits on the town council, works with some of her grandkids to unload our set from boxes. Jackson McSherry walks in, a white 30-something auto mechanic who works down the road—he's got lighting booms borrowed from a local community college in his truck. It's been almost two months since we've worked with these folks on the first annual Milton Street Fair; when we put out a call that we needed volunteers to get the show ready, these and many others came to pitch in.*

At the time of this book's publication, we've gone through this process of research / collaboration / production in Milton, NC, Milton-Freewater, OR, and Milton, MA. We have included here the full script performed in Milton, NC, along with excerpts from the adaptations created for Milton-Freewater, OR and Milton, MA. Milton-Freewater—with its 50% white, 50% Latinx, largely monolingual adult population—required a bilingual script that addressed the town's changing demographics. In Milton, MA, we adapted the script to overtly address issues around race—this Milton was rapidly shifting from having a largely white population of Irish-English descent to one that included Haitian, Eritrean, and Vietnamese immigrants, as well as a growing African American population that was still largely siloed on one side of town.

Following the script of the *MILTON* performance, you'll find a series of essays that chart our course through our time in the Miltons and the relationships we built with each town. Together, they offer a window into our process, our ethics, and our strategies of engagement.

We did this work during a complex span of U.S. history beginning in the "Yes we can/Sí se puede" era of President Obama, and coming to a close during the "Make America Great Again" era of President Trump. We'd been working with people on both sides of this divide—cooking a community dinner with a self-identified Tea Party member one day, and power-washing a building with a liberal Latinx community leader the next. Still, on election night in 2016 we were as blind-sided as many of our other artist friends by this "new" and "divided" country. Political views of all kinds surfaced in our interviews, but we didn't get into heated discussions or debates—it wasn't what we were there to do. Instead, we focused on something everyone we met cared about: the desire to make their town a better place to live.

We talked to people about their lives and our lives, about our play, about what the town needed, and about how art could help them meet those needs. And our project became one of many micro-steps in the continual evolution of the towns. Which, from our point of view, seemed to be an evolution toward more understanding, curiosity, acceptance and trust.

The *MILTON* project taught us not only about the state of our country and our place in it, but also about the ways art can be a catalyst for conversation and action, about the time-scale of change, about the scope of effort it takes to cultivate an audience and build a community, and about what it means to be an American in this country at the beginning of the 21st century.

the play

MILTON

Written & Directed by PearlDamour
Sound Design & Composition: Brendan Connelly
Video & Visual Design: Jim Findlay

Milton, North Carolina

1: Mike Shapiro
2: Vella Lovell
3: Helga Davis

Stage Manager: Miriam Hyfler

Milton, Oregon

1: Todd Jefferson Moore
2: Moises Castro
3: Rose Cano

Translator: Carlos Vargas-Salgado
Stage Manager: Jessilee Marander
Additional Projection Design: Peter Ksander

Milton, Massachusetts

1: Dillon Heape
2: Reya Sehgal
3: Zina Ellis

Co-Director: Emily Mendelsohn
Stage Manager: Miriam Hyfler
Additional Projection Design: Peter Ksander

The full performance text included in this book is the first version of MILTON, created for Milton, NC and performed there in 2013.

The script was adapted for Milton, MA and Milton-Freewater, OR. We've chosen a few selections from the MA and OR scripts to illustrate some of ways in which the script changed from Milton to Milton. These selections can be found in Appendix A on p.101.

the experience

AUDIENCE:
MILTON was performed in the round. Actors began seated in the audience, leaving silence between their first series of lines, evoking a Quaker meeting. They memorized the script but left room for improvisation, especially once they started to get to know people in town and could speak to them directly.

SOUND:
Voice recordings were used throughout the performance, with the recorded voice of an actual Miltonian overtaking the voice of an actor, like channeling a ghost.

MAPS:
Maps of each of the Miltons' downtowns were taped out on the floor in colored spike tape—one layered on top of the other—using the exact orientation of whichever Milton we were performing in. It was at once abstract and specific, allowing actors to point out landmarks during the show.

MODELS:
We incorporated scale models of our performance venues in each Milton as a way of bringing all five Miltons into one room. The models became anchor points for the section in which we describe the demographics, geography, and economy of each town. They were designed and constructed by undergraduate students during a residency we had at Brown University.

SKIES:
Early on we knew we wanted video projections of the sky to be our primary scenic element. Jim Findlay filmed the skies over the towns and designed simple, hanging plexiglass screens for the skies to be projected on. Then he wanted to extend the skies into the space, so he made a cloud out of pillow stuffing and floated it on a helium balloon. It was sweet and kind of magical, floating there in space. And when we put more clouds over the scale model buildings, they formed a miniature sky. Suddenly, the audience was placed up in that sky, looking down at these five towns—a bird's eye view.

casting

We knew we wanted our casts to reflect the racial and ethnic mix of each town in which we were performing. We considered hiring locals to perform, but because our play involved a complex vocal and physical score we decided to cast the show with professional actors.

In North Carolina, the cast consisted of a 40-year-old white man, a 30-year-old woman of African American/Eastern European descent, and a 50-year-old Black woman of Afro-Caribbean descent.

For the North Carolina and Massachusetts shows, we rehearsed in New York with NYC-based performers. For our Oregon show, we rehearsed in Seattle with Seattle-based, bilingual actors—tying it into a teaching residency we had at the University of Washington.

notation

We have tried to give a feeling of the play's music, silence, and overlapping dialogue in the layout of this script.

White space between lines of dialogue indicates silence.

Lines that appears side by side indicates concurrent dialogue—often one performer speaking to the entire audience, while the second actor speaks more quietly to one or two audience members.

Cascading lines with slashes | indicate
         | overlapping lines of dialogue.

Lines in italics indicate singing. Singing is often interlaced with speaking.

Bolded italics indicate stage directions.

Indented pull paragraphs that appear in this font indicate recorded interviews, played through speakers set up in the audience.

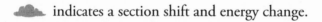 indicates a section shift and energy change.

milton, north carolina

The audience gathers in a small church—a deconsecrated Episcopal church, the current home of the Milton Women's Club. About 70 seats form a kind of hexagon around the playing space. Five plexiglass screens hang above the audience's heads. Simple pedestals stand between the banks of seats, holding small objects gathered from each Milton. There are floor lamps between the banks as well, turned on and off by the actors throughout the performance.

Lisa and Katie come out to greet the audience. They give a brief description of their past work and why they got interested in visiting small towns named Milton. They talk about all five Miltons being underneath one sky.

As they speak, they point to one of the plexiglass screens and say, "This is the sky over Milton, Massachusetts," and the screen comes to life with video of blue sky and white clouds. They continue to call up each Milton's sky, ending with Milton, NC.

When all screens are activated, the show begins.

There are fairly long pauses between each line—Quaker meeting style.

1

Sometimes you are poured a glass of chocolate milk.

2

Sometimes you are served a slice of lemon meringue pie.

3

Sometimes someone gives you a Ziploc bag of kumquats straight from the tree.

1

Sometimes there are three grills going and cracklins in the chip bowl

3

Or it's homemade pulled pork and mashed potatoes.

2

Sometimes you're served a lamb named Elvis for dinner, freshly killed and blessed in the pre-supper blessing, as you stand in the yard under the trees holding hands.

The actors pick up the pace slightly.

3

Sometimes you're invited into the kitchen for lunch: leftover chicken soup with rice and a half turkey sandwich   **2**

Or for dinner with wine made from grapes that grew two miles away.

1

Sometimes a family buys you dinner at the Milton Family Restaurant.

3

Sometimes people call you "bae"   **2**

"Hey bae!"

1

Sometimes people get dressed up for the first visit, but don't bother so much with it for the next one, and that makes you feel welcome.

3

Sometimes you walk in and Ms. Jean Scott exclaims: "But you're so young!"

2

Sometimes you go in through a church door.

1

Sometimes you go in through the side door near the carport.

3

Sometimes you go in through the door of a gymnasium where Kareem Abdul Jabbar played when the gym belonged to Milton College and the Milwaukee Bucks used it for their training camp.

2

A veces usted va a través de una puerta de la biblioteca.

1

Sometimes you go in through the door of the Century 21 Real Estate office on Main Street, then walk down the carpeted hall to the extra office space that the realtors have given to the Americorps volunteer while she works for the town. Her name is Alina, she is originally from Kansas, and she considers herself an "old soul."

3

Sometimes you wonder if people would be opening their doors to you so readily if you weren't two nice-looking white women.

1

Sometimes you discover the place that claims to have invented the cracker.

2

Sometimes your coffee table is the ballot box that got you elected to town council 30 years ago.

1

Sometimes you meet a woman who got just a little bit restless and decided to start a quail farm.

2

Sometimes there is a pair of scissors tattooed gracefully just below the collarbone.

3

They also make hardtack, which is a simple cracker made from water, flour, and, if you're lucky, salt. It was most commonly eaten on long sea voyages, or by soldiers during military campaigns. The manager of this bakery, which is in Milton, Massachusetts, says today they mainly sell it to Civil War reenactors—we met at least one of those in Milton, North Carolina.

1

Sometimes the bartender is wearing a baseball cap that says "Native Pride." And you also see a totem-pole-looking-thing in the bar and you think there must be a connection. But when you ask the bartender, he says the totem pole is just something from a carving competition.

3

Sometimes you know exactly how old a majestic fir tree is because you planted it right there when you moved in.

1

Sometimes you listen to the Praise Choir at High Street Baptist Church.

1

Sometimes you listen to the organ at Milton Presbyterian Church   **3**

                                                        Or at River Zion.

2

Sometimes you sing a hymn with the congregation at Milton Methodist   **3**

                                                        Or at Macedonia.

1

Sometimes the garage is also a woodshop where you make Adirondack chairs out of old skis

        2

        Is where you keep your pecan-shelling machine   **1**

                                                        Is where you keep the town's first fire truck

      3

      Is where you keep your car because you commute to Boston or Quincy

1

(to 3) QuinZEE.

           3

           Right.

2

And your backyard is where you keep your horses   **1**

           Keep your pet pig   **3**

           Install your solar panels

    1

    Have your St. Patrick's Day parties   **3**

           Plant your vegetable garden.

1

Sometimes there are paintings of people who
look like ancestors on the wall, and you find out
that the people who own the house actually don't
know who they are.

    2

    There are photographs of your in-laws on the
wall that you are finally letting yourself take
down because your husband's last sister just
passed away.

3

Sometimes you meet the man who laid all the sidewalks in town   **2**

    And sometimes you meet
someone whose parents built the
first mosque in New England.

3

And sometimes you are most proud of hitting a kid so hard on the football field that you broke his collarbone.

1

Sometimes you go to Catholic Mass on Easter Sunday and hear the priest tell a joke that ends with the punchline "ta dah!"

2

Sometimes there is no bar.

3

Sometimes they started another town just across the tracks to put the bars in.

1

Sometimes you hear stories about drinking Sam Adams out of 350-year-old silver goblets loaned to the church for a centennial celebration.

3

Sometimes you share in chocolates shaped like liquor bottles with real liquor inside.

2

Sometimes you find a weather station that has been there for 100 years, and every day of those 100 years someone has recorded a reading of the weather by hand.

3

Sometimes the tire repair shop is also the diner

2

And the museum is also where you pay your water bill.

1

Sometimes you meet a man who moved to Eastern Oregon from Nigeria to be priest of a Catholic Church whose congregation is primarily Latino.

2

Sometimes you watch a grown woman blush when you ask her where the mystery is in her life.

Harmonic tones fill the space. The projection screens glow five different colors of blue: abstracted squares of sky. The skies remain on through the upcoming song.

3

Sometimes someone drives you to Simco's in Mattapan for Fried Clams.

1

Sometimes someone drives you to edge of town so you can see the new stretch of interstate that will bypass Milton.

2

Sometimes you are given a driving tour of things that aren't actually there:

1

The canning center where you could bring your vegetables to preserve them for the winter

Music underscoring begins.

2

The old post office that used to be in Miss Nola's house

3

The sugar mill was right there in that empty lot.

1

And next door was the grain mill

The actors begin to sing.

2

The grain mill.

3

The old church with a door that faced down Main Street.

1 & 2

It was the first thing you'd see when you rode into town.

3

The old church was in the parking lot of the new church.

2

That car wash was   **3**

The Dog and Suds, the movie theater   **ALL**

And then Mr. Lipscomb's General Store

2

With the crystal dishes filled with penny candy.

1 & 2

And over there—the Old Hotel—

3

That burned down | in a fire.

1 | *The Soda Fountain that is now a* | *bar*

3 | The depot that is now a
restaurant called The Depot.

2

The apple orchard.

3

The little green church   **1**

There are still some apple orchards around here   **3**

You'd pick 'em and bring
the crates to the cannery
that was right over there.

1

And then   **3**

The pea farm   **ALL**

The Academy for Girls   **2**

that opened in 1820   **3**

Actually it was called
Milton Female Academy.

3

The dance hall   **1**

Where we used to dance the Cajun Waltz.

3

The College   **2**

Milton College went bankrupt in 1982.

1

The football field for the college.

ALL

The cotton gin, the GM plant

A flurry of overlapping spoken text:

1

And there was a school for Black children before integration right at the end of Bridge
Street

2

The original Baptist Church, Milton Baptist, burned | down in 1975

3 | And the house everyone called Longwood
burned down just last year

1

And the Tap and Dye was a   **2**

Convenience Store   **3**

Oh right they had the best chicken salad

3   **1**

En los primeros días, los trabajadores migrantes   And why did the Gas Station close?
se plantaba su carpa a la derecha en esta esquina,
donde las casas eran, y hacím fuego para cocinar   **2**
los alimentos después de un día de trabajo.

Regulations? Too expensive to upgrade
the pumps?

1

And wasn't there a   **2**

Tomato canning factory yes and a   **1**

Library built by Carnegie

2

That's still there, on Main Street, but it's not a library anymore.

Singing resumes.

3

Farmland   **1**

Subdivision

2

Called Sugarmill Pond.

3
Farmland   **1**
    Middle School   **2**
        One of the best in Lafayette Parish.

3
Farmland   **1**
    Whole blocks of houses.   **2**
        Farmland   **2**
          Leased for horses.   **ALL**
           Farmland, still farmland.

2
But the guy who farms it is not from around here.

3
Sometimes you hear a story of a bridge in
Milton, Louisiana that had to be turned to
the side manually, using a crank, by the bridge
master and his five children, so boats could
navigate the Vermilion River.

1
(Indicating the map on the floor) It runs right
through here—starting at Bayou Fusilier, which
is fed by Bayou Teche.

> **Lights begin to dim. The sky screens
> shift to dark blue night sky. 3 is
> standing near a lamp. She switches it
> on. She is illuminated in the dark, with
> the night skies moving above her.**

2
Sometimes you are sitting next to that river, in a
bar, when you hear that story.

3
You are sitting at a bar, outside actually, on the
back deck, at a picnic table, in the dark, it's
night, it's a cool night and you're sitting with the

1
Cypress trees.

3 (cont)

bar owner, who is known as Wawee, and his bar is called Wawee's On The River. Through the darkness you can see his gray handlebar mustache hanging down in an impressive curl past his chin. He may be telling you something about being a Libertarian. He may be telling you something about how his uncle used to own this bar.

1 (cont)

Egrets.
The sound of frogs . . .

A fishing boat or two.
Or maybe a pirogue, which is flat-bottomed canoe.

3

He may be telling you something about his brother who has a welding shop just four blocks that way, a shop which to you looks like an artistic wonderland of wrought iron sculptures, but to someone else might seem like an eyesore. This is Cajun country—families are tight here. He may be telling you about his 98-year-old mother Nola, who lives with him and his daughter Rennie. He may be telling you about how, when there's a big rain in Milton, he watches the river to see how fast it's "coming up," and how, if the rain keeps coming, people start calling him to ask if he needs help putting the juke box or the pool table and the beer cooler up on cinder blocks. He may be telling you that Rennie is short for Serenity, or about how someone has killed all but one of the geese that swim out back behind his bar—maybe alligators, or maybe the Mexican construction workers who were working nearby—he thinks they killed them for food. And he may tell you about how he thinks that one goose swims around calling out all the time, and he thinks it's lonely, he thinks it is calling out for its mate, he thinks the goose sometimes mistakes one of the old wooden pylons sticking up out of the river for its mate, and then he may say to you, "Come on, come see" and lead you across the deck, under the awning and back into the building, past the people playing pool, behind the cement bar, through the swinging door to a little storage room where there is a cage rigged up with heat lamps. And inside the cage you see—is it seven yellow baby ducks? And two or three baby geese? That he is feeding and nurturing so that when they are big enough, he can release them so that one lonely goose has some friends.

1, 2, and 3 perform "Sky Humming 1"—an extended moment of wordless singing. They look up and watch night skies move across the screens. As the sky humming ends, screens shift to a bright daytime sky, filled with light clouds.

1

Sometimes, when you ask Nola, Wawee's mother, how she got the job running the post office out of her living room, she says something like:

1 continues speaking as he places his hand on a speaker. We hear Nola's actual voice speaking with 1 for a moment, then the recording carries on alone:

NOLA: And uh, you pull the right strings, you know, sometimes.

KATIE: Yeah, yeah.

NOLA: And you can—there was no jobs. I graduated high school in nineteen thirty—oh, thirty one.

WAWEE: The Depression

KATIE + LISA: Uh huh . . .

NOLA: That was a loooong time ago.

KATIE + LISA: Yeah.

NOLA: And here in Milton—Milton is big now, considering what it was at that time.

KATIE + LISA: Mm hm.

NOLA'S CHILDHOOD FRIEND: I knew . . . one Protestant Republican. My first grade teacher. Otherwise you were Democrat and Catholic. *(Laughter)* One pulpit Republican.

LISA: Um, Nola? I was asking George yesterday—how did you meet your husband?

NOLA: My husband was about ten years older than me.

LISA: Uh huh.

NOLA: And, uh. There was nobody. Uh, we just—we lived in the same town—

LISA: You just knew each other—

NOLA: We were raised together!

LISA: Mm hm.

NOLA: So for a good while he tried courting me. I mean, he'd come—and my dad was—it's like we were talking about politicians? My husband would visit my dad at home, talking politics, and I guess—he'd want to bring me, take me to the movie . . . well, and I'd say, well I don't want to go. I didn't want to see him because I thought he was too old for me! And it took him a long time to get me to go!

>*Everyone laughs.*

Finally, being that you didn't meet anybody, there was no one coming into Milton . . . I was out of school and he was working, so he had a car and . . . so every once in a while, well, we'd take my sister and her friend, and we'd go to the movie or we'd have supper somewhere. And so that's how we just started going together, once in a while. And finally, we . . . eventually got married . . .

The daytime skies continue for a moment in silence.

1
Sometimes you realize that the most you will ever get is a glimpse   **2**

                                                   A piece   **3**

                                                        Of the whole picture.

The skies turn off. The lamps remain on.

☁

2

Sometimes you watch an old man expertly stitch a sole onto a boot using a machine called a shoe-stitcher | that was in Milton Freewater. Look. *(Takes out her phone to show the video to someone.)*

  3 | Sometimes there are four giant vats being prepared in the firehouse to cook a "Fireman's Stew." | Here's a picture.

  2 | Sometimes you meet two women who decided to start a pet cemetery. | I have pictures, here.

  1 | And in the pet cemetery | there is a grave for a dog named Short Stuff, and on the grave is a cement statue of a black puppy with a pink pedicure holding a lantern in its mouth. Look at this picture.

  3 | Sometimes in the elementary school cookbook there are four different recipes for Crawfish Fettuccine. *(Hands someone the cookbook.)*

2

Sometimes in the basement there is a secret tavern that was frequented by men in a dry county | in the 1930s. I have a picture right here.

  1 | Sometimes the best birthday present is a belt equipped with camouflage Koozies that can hold six beers. A picture—pass that around.

2

Sometimes there is Norteño music playing, and a stand with a woman selling Elephant Ears. | *(2 puts her hand on the speaker and Norteño music plays under the following.)*

  1 | Elephant Ears are like fry bread, with lots of cinnamon sugar. | I have a picture.

  3 | On the blue bowling alley T-shirt is a picture of a happy bowling pin holding a pizza and a beer. *(Hands someone the T-shirt.)*

2

Sometimes there is a ceramic rabbit on the table with fur carved so perfectly it looks like it's made out of icing. A picture—look.

1

Sometimes there is a calendar on the wall of the diner from the local funeral home that shows a bevy of quail | making their way through the woods. Here's a picture.
> **3** | On the shelf is a hand towel woven out of brown cotton grown in southern Louisiana. *(Hands someone the handmade towel.)*

>> **1**
>> In the basement there is an artist studio filled with a miniature rendition of the Alamo. | Look at this picture.
>>> **2** | And the man who made it helped invent Dungeons and Dragons, and also plays bass at the Methodist Church. | Here's a photo of Uncle Duke.
>>>> **1** | On the end table there is a framed photo of a husband wearing his favorite shirt, and his wife is standing before you wearing an apron made out of that very same shirt. | Here's a picture.

Norteño music fades.

>>> **2** | Sometimes a man comes back to the dinner party and has you sit and listen to a song that he feels explains his worldview.

2 puts her hand on the speaker and the country song "The Journey of Your Life" by Jake Owen plays. The actors pause to sing along for a moment, then turn it off.

3

In the pocket of the Carhartt Overalls are some handmade earrings made by the man wearing the Carhartt Overalls. *(Hands someone the earrings.)*

1

On the table is a coffee mug from the Milton Family Restaurant. *(Hands someone the mug.)*

2

We ate there with the Richardson family after church. The restaurant is run by Abib Zonuzi. His citizenship certificate hangs in a frame by the cash register.

3

Outside the Art Gallery is the Women's Club Bake | Sale—

        1 | At the street fair food court is High Street's | Fish Fry—

        3 | Where you can buy Moe's Famous | Pound Cake—

        1 | Where you can buy Amanda's Famous Honey Bun Cake—

        ALL

        Here are some pictures!

1

On the side of the street there is a statue of a frog climbing a telephone pole   **2** Of a frog stitching an American flag

    3

    De una rana sosteniendo una hucha   **2** Of a frog lying on his | stomach, reading a book—

        3 | Her

        ALL

        We have pictures of those!

1

Sometimes, in every house you go to, there is an old clock ticking its way through your conversation.

    1 places hand on a speaker and we hear a clock ticking under the following.

2

On the shelf is a piece of pottery fired in a kiln just | a few miles away. *(Hands someone the vase.)*

    3 | In the living room are four big saddles on display. | You can pass that around.

    2 | On the wall above the cash register

in the pizza place is a painted mural of people eating pizza and if you turn your head, you might meet the people who are in the mural right now! Here's a picture.

1

In the refrigerator is a glass bottle of chocolate milk from Thatcher Family Farms. *(Hands someone the bottle.)* We met | Maritta Cronin, whose family started the farm in 1891.

2 | In a case in the museum is Joseph Goodrich's personal toothpick. If you were rich, you had your own. If you were poor, you shared one with the other men at the table. *(Hands someone a replica of Joseph Goodrich's personal toothpick.)* Don't worry, it's not the real thing.

Clock ticking out.

3

In the rack by the front door are brochures advertising the now-defunct Milton College. *(Hands out brochures.)*

1

On the folding table, next to the stack of handmade soap, is a CD of music by Anne Haley. **3**

It sounds like this. *(3 puts her hand on speaker and Anne Haley's "It's a Beautiful Life" begins to play.)*

2

In the house on Broad Street are pieces of furniture made in the 1800s by a free Black cabinet-maker named Thomas Day. Here are some pictures.

3

Sometimes, there is a bright blue house | on the main drag and inside is a Chinese American woman who runs an artisanal chocolate shop.

3 shares some chocolates from Petit Noirs chocolate shop with a group of audience members.

1

On the wall of the elementary school is a hand-painted mural of a globe, whales, and other wild animals with the words, "There's no place like Milton." Here's a picture.

Anne Haley's music fades out.

2

In the office of the cemetery manager is a booklet listing the inscriptions of every grave marker in the cemetery. *(Hands someone the booklet.)*

1

On the sign outside the corner store are plastic letters arranged to say, "Success is not final, failure is not fatal." Here's a picture.

2

In the back room of the house was the Orchard Beauty Shop. We met Al, whose mom ran the shop, at the Varsity Bowl in Wisconsin. *(Hands someone a T-shirt from the bowling alley.)*

1

On the shelf of the thrift store called Blue Mountain Treasures is a pair of salt-and-pepper shakers from Washington state shaped like grizzly bears. *(Hands out the grizzly bears.)*

Music underscoring begins.

2

On the main street next to the old bank is a house purchased out | of a Sears Catalog.

                             1 | And another, across from the college, purchased from Montgomery Ward.

The actors begin to sing. They pass out a few more photos of things they name during the song.

2

And the house with the window   **3**

                           Taken from the old school.

1

We saw a framed photo of the Obama family   **2**

                                       Sitting on a table next to Cleota, a Black woman who's spent every one of her 90 years in Milton.

3
And a framed photo of the new pope **1**

In the guest room of the Duhon's house, who live four blocks from their Catholic Church.

2
And sometimes at the end of the interview someone gives you **3**

A jar of fig preserves **1**

A book about the Dan River. And sometimes

3
A T-shirt from their Bowling Alley

2
A T-shirt from their Biker Club

2
And sometimes you walk into the convention center and find **3**

The stage decorated for Cowboy Church.

1
Or someone shows you **2**

A hand-painted heart in the closet **3**

From the previous owner's child.

1
Or someone stops and explains that **2**

The strangely shaped ladders leaning up against the wall

3

Son para recoger las cerezas.

1
You might see a giant blade from a windmill **2**

Lying in the middle of the field

3

And then sometimes   **2**

Next to the cash register there is a catalog   **3**

To buy Quinceañera dresses

2

Or embroidered shirts, or big silver belt buckles.

1

And in the museum, on the second floor are   **2+3**

Tiny flowers made out of human hair.

2

We also saw those in a frame on the wall of the pecan farmers' house in Louisiana.

3

In the bar is a young army veteran   **1**

Showing off his pink wig   **2**

He bought for / Halloween.

1+2

On the front lawn

3

Is a wheelchair—decked out with party lights and a sound system.

Sky screens glow to life: Milton-Freewater sky. Bright blue, gorgeous clouds.

2

In the wheelchair sits John Perkins, the official Santa Claus of Milton-Freewater, OR.

1

Sometimes, you get invited to Santa's house on the edge of town: he wants to show you his favorite view, which is actually in his front yard. You are sitting in his front yard, in lawn chairs that he pulled out from under his RV, which is in the driveway right next to you. You are sitting in his front yard, looking out over the Blue Mountains—

1

The Blue Mountains are in the distance, stretching across the horizon—with not much between you and them except low-lying land and sky.

2

Just down the highway from Santa John, about a five-minute drive, is Freewater Park.

Sometimes, on the first weekend in May, you will find a Cinco de Mayo festival in that park.

3

If you're sitting there, the Blue Mountains would be that way, on this side of Milton-Freewater, and on this side are hills they call the Palouse, which people farm. So the town is in a gentle valley.

Wide open space. Acres of Vineyards. Orchards. Farm Equipment. Horses.

(Indicating the map on the floor) Right about here. There's a pool, and the middle school is somewhere this way.

Booths selling tacos, Elephant Ears . . . a stage for music and dancing.

1

Santa may be telling you that this view is the reason he moved here. The house is nothing special, but when he turned around and saw it, he knew he had found his home.

2

Sometimes, while you are at the festival, you start talking with Mayra Osorio, one of the festival organizers. She might be telling you about how the festival got started, or about her five kids, or about how she makes her living as a hospice worker.

1

He may be telling you about why he is in a wheelchair: because of nerve damage probably caused by

Agent Orange when he was in Vietnam. He first started passing through Milton on his way to the VA hospital in Walla Walla. He may look over at you with his big white beard and dark sunglasses and start telling you about his frustrations with politicians, saying—

1 places his hand on a speaker, so we hear Santa John's actual voice speaking with 1 for the first sentence. Then the recording carries on alone.

SANTA JOHN: I'm sitting out here, I've got a VA pension and social security/disability, and I haven't gotten a raise in almost four years. And yet: how many raises have they had? So it's more of a selfish thing. They're taking care of themselves. And they're so worried that someone coming into the country illegal is going to take something away from someone who wants to earn it. Walla Walla and Milton-Freewater have some of the best employment opportunities for anybody. Working in the fields, working in the orchards. I set here, and I go to these orchards, and how many Anglos are in those orchards? The owner. That's it. He doesn't want Americans in there. And the reason he doesn't want it is they think they deserve all the opportunities and yet they're not willing to work for it. That's that selfish thing coming back again.

2

At the festival you may ask Mayra if she works out of her home.

2 continues speaking as she turns on a speaker, so we hear Mayra's actual voice speaking with 2 for the first sentence. Then the recording carries on alone.

MAYRA: I go into homes. I used to manage a nursing home that was for Alzheimer's—the final stage of Alzheimer's. I've been nursing—like caregiving?—since I was 15 and I'm 31. So I've been doing it for a while. So just . . . just . . . doing the final stages . . . kind of fulfills me. Because I can give them that peace and that lifestyle that they really deserve. The other fulfillment I get is that I can give the families that peace of mind. You know—you can go. Go, get a break. I'm right here, everything's gonna go fine. So I'm able to give them and deliver them that calm. That: Don't worry about it. Yeah, like: We got this. And if she goes, she goes, you know?

SANTA JOHN: I had a kid down here, 17 years old. He stopped by the house the other day. We were chatting. He says, "John," he says, "I think me and my girlfriend are going to get married." And I said, "Well before you do that you gotta have a job." And he said, "OK, what do I do?" And I said, "Well I tell you what I would do. Is I would go down to Wal-Mart because you want to be home during the day, and uh, stock shelves."

LISA: Just 'cause he likes being home during the day?

SANTA JOHN: Yeah him and his girlfriend like to hang out together. So he goes over there, and he comes back and stops by the next day. And he says, "John, I got a job." And I said, "What are your hours?" "3-11." I said, "Is that good?" He said, "It's the best thing that ever happened." First real job he ever had. He didn't think he would ever get a job at the Wal-Mart. His uncles, his cousins, out of four people, three of them are double felons. And he's not. And I told him: "You can't put yourselves in their footsteps. You get in there, you work your butt off for 40-50 hours a week, and then you eventually move yourself up." He said, "Yeah I gotta get myself my GED." And I just looked him square in the eye and said, "That's what I had to do . . . "

ASHLEY: What do you feel you learned about death from doing this kind of work?

MAYRA: About death? Um, I feel like death is a graduation. I feel like death is a graduation. And I feel like sometimes people need to just know that they have been loved and it's OK, and that love will continue. It's not going to go. It's not like nobody cares. Sometimes the prayers are what they need also. Just to feel that peace in their heart. So I feel like, the violence of it is life at the time that they're living. There is something that was meant to be. So I try to do my best.

The performers begin to hum again, as the projection screens come alive with sky. This goes on for a few moments, then skies and humming cease.

2
Sometimes your job is to manage people's money.

3

Sometimes your job is to clean people's houses.

1

Sometimes your job is to be a teaching assistant at the middle school.

2

Sometimes your job is to inspect pipelines out in the Gulf of Mexico.

3

Sometimes your job is to teach new mothers about breast-feeding.

1

Parfois, votre travail consiste à aider les nouveaux immigrants s'acclimater à leur ville natale.

3

Sometimes your job is to organize Oldies Night, a listening hour at the library.

2

Sometimes your job is to sell pastries and tortillas at the panadería.

> *The energy picks up as the actors begin moving through the space, pointing to individual audience members and assigning jobs. It is direct and sometimes hilarious.*

1

Your job is to serve beers.

2

Your job is to sell space on billboards.

3

Your job is to weld deep flow tanks.

1

Your job is to embalm bodies.

2

Your job is to fix people's air conditioners.

3

Your job is to teach home education.

1

Your job is to teach math to middle school students.

2

Your job is to check people out at the grocery store.

1

Your job is to harvest tobacco.

2

Your job is to be the assistant principal of the elementary school.

3

Your job is to read the gauges on oil rigs out in the Gulf.

1

Your job is raise quail.

3

Your job is to raise kids.

3

Now, it's trickier because of Common Core—you need to get the students to draw diagrams and think conceptually, OK? Because there are tests at the state and federal level, here's some information . . . *(Hands out a pamphlet.)*

1

There's not really a handbook for that, but I think there are experts—in this section, how many of you have raised kids? OK great, so if

3

Your job is to run a ballet school.

2

Your job is to sell and repair pool equipment.

3

Your job is to run the youth center, which includes running the fundraising campaign to renovate the youth center.

1

Your job is to raise cows.

2

Your job is to work at Lowe's. *(Hands someone a name tag.)* Here's your name tag, your hours are 7am to 4, OK?

1

Your job is to be the mayor.

2

Su trabajo es ser el gerente del bar.

3

Your job is to be a contractor, until you fall off your own porch and break your ankle.

1

Your job is to be a long distance trucker.

2

Your job is to be the parish priest.

1

Your job is to deliver the milk.

you all could meet with them after the show and give some tips that would be great.

2

Yes, it sounds old-fashioned, but Thatcher Farms

3

Your job is to be a dentist.
Your job is to be a dental assistant.

1

Your job is to run the bowling alley.
Your job is to read the water meters.

3

Your job is to work at the canning factory until the canning factory closes.

2

Your job is to make and sell fish sandwiches at the street fair. You have to apprentice with Shirley and Ronnie Wilson because they're really good at it.

3

Your job is to sell Sprint network telephones in an area where the Sprint coverage isn't actually so great.

1

Your job is to practice employment law, and make puppets out of newspaper when you retire.

2

Your job is to be the town manager.

1

Your job is to run Sam's Corner Store.

1

Your job is Equine Massage. Don't worry, you are going to find it really rewarding. There's nothing like feeling a horse's knotted muscles relax in your hands.

Dairy has been around a long time and still delivers its milk in glass bottles so you need to take care, OK? Here's the keys to your truck. *(Hands someone a ring of keys.)*

2

Just when Elmer Stewart is on vacation.

2

Your job is to entertain people by singing Cowboy Ballads.

2

Your job is to work directing cars at the racetrack   **1**

Right over there.

2

Your job is to assist Shirley Cadmus at the art gallery   **1**

Right across the street.

2

Your job is to run the pizza place   **1**

And your job is to serve pizza at the pizza place. You will apprentice with Gwen at Aunt Millie's, she will teach you how to make pizza with lots and lots of cheese.

3

Your job is to work at the GM plant until . . . well, you know.

1

Su trabajo consiste en cocinar la comida en el restaurante.

2

Your job is to change and repair tires   **1**

Oh, but sometimes you will need to duck behind the counter to cook up some burgers, because you work at the Milton Tire and Grill.

2

Your job is to clean the post office on Sundays. Because Nancy Hughes needs to rest!

1

Your job is to run the heating oil company.

2

Your job is to work the front counter at the vineyards, selling people wine tastings and talking to them about wine.

3

Which have taken over since all the pea farms moved to South America.

2

Your job is to own a cherry orchard.

1

(Pointing to a white person) Your job is to pick the cherries.   **3**

(Pointing to a person of color) It's more likely that that would be your job.

2

Your job is to distribute the cherries.

1

Your job is to work in the bank   **3**

But that's two towns over, there are no banks in your town.

2

(Pointing to a Black person) Your job is to work in the Goodyear Factory   **3**

Unless you don't get the job because you are "overqualified."

1

Sometimes a town that farmed peas has to reinvent itself as a town that farms grapes.

3 brings a model of the Milton-Freewater Community Building into the playing space.

3
This is the Community Building in Milton-Freewater, Oregon, the building where we will be performing this show.

A harmonic tone fills the space. The actors look up to see the sky screens shift to show Oregon sky.

2
Milton-Freewater, Oregon is 2,621 miles from this room.

1 walks around the stage, showing the model to the audience.

1
Milton-Freewater was created when the towns of Milton and Freewater merged. Milton came first, but it was a dry town, so Freewater was created, in part, to put the bars in. The Community Building is situated on the Freewater side of town right about . . . here. On Northeast 5th Street.

1 places the model on the map on the floor.

3
Sometimes a town known for factory work has to reinvent itself in ways it is still figuring out.

2 brings a scale model of the Milton House Museum into the playing space.

2
This is the Milton House Museum in Milton, Wisconsin, the building where we will be performing this show.

A harmonic tones fills the space. The actors look up to see the sky screens shift to show Wisconsin sky.

3

Milton, Wisconsin is 869 miles from this room.

2 walks around the stage, showing the model to the audience.

2

The Milton House Museum was once the home of Joseph Goodrich, who settled Milton—his home was also a hotel, and a stop on the Underground Railroad. Goodrich named the town after John Milton because he considered it "Paradise Found." The Milton House is situated right about . . . here, on South Janesville Street.

2 places the model on the map on the floor.

3

Sometimes a town that never incorporated still feels like a town, even though it is slowly being absorbed into Lafayette.

1 brings a scale model of the Milton Civic Center into the playing space.

1

This is the Civic Center in Milton, Louisiana, the building where we will be performing this show.

A harmonic tone fills the space. The actors look up to see the sky screens shift to show Louisiana sky.

2

Milton, Louisiana is 981 miles from this room.

1 walks around the stage, showing the model to the audience.

1

Milton is a Cajun town in Southeast Louisiana. The doctor who used to administer to the Cajun families in the late 1800s named it after himself. The Civic Center is in Picard Park on the edge of town, right about here.

1 places the model on the map on the floor.

2

Sometimes a town with a history of being wealthy and white starts an organization called "Citizens for a Diverse Milton."

3 holds a scale model of the Milton Public Library.

3

This is the public library in Milton, Massachusetts, the building where we will be performing this show.

A harmonic tone fills the space. The actors look up to see the sky screens shift to show Massachusetts sky.

1

Milton, Massachusetts is 690 miles from this room.

3 walks around the stage, showing the model to the audience.

3

This is by far the biggest Milton we've been visiting—it's about 25,000 people, and while it's known as a suburb of Boston, it still very much has its own identity. This Milton recently celebrated its 350th anniversary. The public library is situated about right here, in the center of town, at the intersection of Reedsdale Road and Canton Avenue.

3 places the model on the map on the floor.

1

Sometimes a town that farmed tobacco has to reinvent itself as a town known for museums and shops.

2 brings a scale model of the Milton Women's Club into the playing space.

2

This is the Women's Club, where we are performing this show right now.

1

Milton is one of the oldest towns in North Carolina, founded in . . . *(Audience answers: 1796!)*

2

The Women's Club is situated on the corner of Academy and Broad Streets, right about here.

> ***2 hands the model to 3, who places it on the map on the floor.***

3

Milton, North Carolina is right here.

> ***A harmonic tone fills the space. The actors look up to see the sky screens shift to North Carolina sky.***

1

Sometimes, you visit five towns named Milton and in every single one, someone tells you they wish people would stop fighting so much.

3

Sometimes, you visit five towns named Milton and in every single one, someone tells you about a place they go to "get away from it all." And you wonder: what's everyone trying to get away from?

2

Sometimes, you visit five towns named Milton and in all of them you meet people who are the descendants of farmers, but most of them don't have farms anymore.

1

Sometimes you visit five towns named Milton and in three of them the downtown areas are a combination of empty buildings and second-hand stores.

3

Sometimes you visit five towns named Milton and one of them has rebranded itself as "Muddy Frogwater Country," and most of the businesses in town have statues of frogs doing chores that relate to their business. And when you ask if the area is famous for frogs, they tell you no, not really, Muddy Frogwater is a nickname for the town that may have been created by a bunch of drunk kids.

1

Sometimes you drive up to the Chapel Specialties Building to meet Jim and Linda Lyke in Milton, Wisconsin.

The skies all shift to Wisconsin sky.

2

It's an old church that has been chopped up into a coffee house, shops, small businesses. You notice the sky as you duck in the front door. Sometimes Jim and Linda take you down the staircase, past the community board, past Kelly Richardson's office where she practices brain integration physical therapy . . . until you get to a room that people can sign out for meetings . . . the door is open and no one is in there, so you flick on the lights and settle around the table to talk. Sometimes a conversation that starts off about raising kids turns into a conversation about faith and God, and you decide to ask—

3

(indicating map) Right about here, not too far from the Milton House—

High ceilings—

Stained glass windows.

2 puts her hand on a speaker and we hear the actual recording.

KATIE: Can I ask you a question that might be too personal?

LINDA LYKE: Yeah. Yeah—yeah.

KATIE: I'm just curious about . . . I come from a Jewish family, but very secular, my parents did not raise me to be religious. And what is that experience of hearing what God is telling you, what is that like? Because I'm wondering if it's the same as my experience of really trying to listen to my instinct without my brain telling me "you should do this, you should do that." Is there a way to describe it?

LINDA: Um, well—I spend a lot of time in prayer. And I make sure to read the Bible every day, and I've had God tell me things through reading the Bible. And I can just tell—when I have that sense of emotion wash over me and I'm reading something it's like: Okay, that's what I'm supposed to do. Or like . . . I don't have, people have said they've heard God's voice—our pastor, actually Pastor George has said that. I've never had that, but I have had, and you've had this too, where a sense of peace washes over you while you're praying about something and you're like "Okay, thank you, now I get what I'm supposed to do here." So it's more, it's more, um, it's more . . . discipline. If I'm making sure that I pray, and reading the Bible regularly, it's where you build on, it's just like exercise, you can't just all of a sudden have faith. It's something that you build on. And it becomes a part of who you are. Because you don't just pick up the Bible and understand it.

KATIE: I um, yeah, that notion of practice, I think is so important and it just strikes me that today my answer of advice for future generations might be if you want to do something, you have to practice it. Because I feel like one thing that is happening is the expectation is that I can have it now, I can get it now or I don't need to put in the time of re-meeting yourself again and again.

LINDA: I agree. And I do think that's that sense of, I don't know if you want to call it entitlement, but a lot of young people . . .

LISA: It's interesting to me that . . . um, I grew up Catholic and my Dad teaches at a Black Catholic—oh he's, um, an administrator at a Black Catholic University called Xavier in New Orleans. And he, um, my parents both go to church all the time, and um, he has a very personal relationship to prayer. And just as you described that to me, it's so interesting that it's about developing a personal relationship to the Bible. But also, um, how body-related it is, when you feel like you're hearing God's word. That it's

visceral—it's a feeling in your body.
LINDA: It is. Absolutely.

LISA: It's just—

On the recording we hear the sound of someone poking their head in the room.

JIM: Are you guys closing up?

WORKER: We are.

ALL: OK!

WORKER: Uh—do you guys—is this a reserved room or something?

ALL: Nope! Sorry! We're just—

LISA: We're just squatting, as you might say . . .

The actors begin to hum again, under the Wisconsin skies. This continues for a long moment. The humming ends. The skies dissolve into color fields and continue to glow.

1
Sometimes you meet someone who believes that everything happens | for a reason
2 | You meet someone who believes that everything is random.

3
Sometimes you meet someone who believes that | it's important to go to college
1 | You meet someone who believes it's important to work with your hands.

2

Sometimes you believe it's important to be | happy

                                3 | We are all here to suffer.

1

You believe the right answer is in | the struggle

                        2 | We were created for God's | pleasure

                                      3 | We are all in a play, and the
                                            writer is | God

                                                1 | We're all out here on our
                                                    own, and the universe is one
                                                    big improvisation.

2

You believe that the government shouldn't get involved with a rancher who has been running cattle on a piece of land for 25 years.

3

You believe the Mexican immigrants in your town   **1**

                                        Are illegal   **2**

                                                  No human being is illegal

                  3

Are simply following in the footsteps of the British settlers who were dissatisfied with their lot and decided to | settle in a new place

                                2 | decided to take over another country where people had
                                          already been living for hundreds of years.

The actors begin assigning beliefs, pointing to individual audience members.

1
You believe the state line between Oregon and Washington should have been drawn vertically instead of horizontally.

2
You believe the integration of the schools was handled really poorly in the late '60s, and actually caused a great deal of damage to race relations in your town.

3
You believe all you have are your relationships with people and the legacy of how you lived your life.

1
You believe you can fall into complacency and conformity any time, so when you are young you need to follow your dreams.

2
You believe following your dreams is way easier for some people than others.

3
You believe that life begins at conception.

1
You believe that life begins when the fetus's heart starts beating.

2
You believe that access to birth control is a necessary right for men and women.

3
Usted cree que la producción de manzanas es importante y que los estudiantes deben estudiar y valor de producción agrícola.

2

You believe this world, it's rough man, and we gotta be in this big bad world together.

1

You believe you should teach your children about death.

2

You believe Black people and women are still at a disadvantage when it comes to jobs and education.

3

You believe they should stop whining, they won their battles a long time ago.

1

You believe someone who says, "I'm not racist, but" is about to say something racist.

2

You believe that the universe is moving towards awareness and that each one of us is part of moving forward.

3

You believe that gay people exist and should be allowed to be themselves.

1

You believe that gay people are unnatural and should be turned straight.

2

You don't even like those words "gay" and "straight" and are trying to find a new language for it all.

1

(to 2) What do you mean "it all"?

2

(to 1) I mean "IT ALL."

3

You believe in ghosts.

1

You believe people should pull themselves up by their bootstraps.

2

You believe someone should sell bootstraps.

3

You believe someone should give away bootstraps for free.

1

You believe in gun control　**2**

　　　　　　　　　　　You believe in some gun control　**3**

　　　　　　　　　　　　　　　　　　　You believe in the right to bear
　　　　　　　　　　　　　　　　　　　arms　**2**

　　　　　　　　　　　　　　　　　　　　　　　I have bare arms　**3**

　　　　　　　　　　　　　　　　　　　　　　　　　　　Stop it.

1

You believe undocumented Mexican immigrants are sucking up our country's resources.

3

You believe undocumented Mexican | immigrants are doing jobs that white people simply refuse to
do anymore.　　　　　　　　　　**2** | Usted cree que los inmigrantes indocumentados están
　　　　　　　　　　　　　　　　　　haciendo trabajos que los blancos simplemente se niegan a
　　　　　　　　　　　　　　　　　　hacerlo nunca más.

1

You believe people should take better care of the cemetery.

2

You believe that everyone's on the earth to be part of one big puzzle that adds up to you're not exactly
sure what.

3

You believe it's important to spread joy.

1

You believe you should lock your doors.

2

You believe if you can help somebody, you should help them.

3

You believe that the world is a scarier place now than it was 50 years ago.

2

You believe the world is more free than it was 50 years ago.

1

You believe that we live in a big country that was built for people to live side by side, and live out many points of view   **3**

         But you don't want to be in the room with all of them.

1

You believe that we live in a big country that was built for people to live side by side, and live out many points of view   **2**

         But you don't know how to be in the room with all of them.

3

You believe that we live in a big country that was built for people to live side by side, and live out many points of view   **1**

         But you are afraid to be in the room with all of them.

2

You believe that we live in a big country that was built for people to live side by side, and live out many points of view   **3**

         But you don't have time to be in the room with all of them.

1
You believe that we live in a big country that was built for people to live side by side, and live out many points of view **2**

But you wonder what it would be like to be in
the room | with all of them.
3 | To be in the | room with all of them
1 | To be in the room with all of them.
2
To be in | the room
3 | To be in the | room
ALL | To be in the room.

2 places her hand on a speaker, and we hear the voice of Diane Biggs, a Milton-Freewater, OR elder, telling us about her philosophy of the universe. 1 and 3 activate the other two speakers, and other voices, old and young, of many races, speak of their lives and beliefs, and of the towns as they were, are, and might be.

As the collage of voices grows more dense, the actors gently carry out small, handheld clouds made of pillow stuffing and attached with fish line to helium balloons. The actors "float" the clouds over the scale models of the buildings from the five Miltons, creating a sky that holds them all.

As the collage of voices recedes, each actor goes to a section of audience chairs. Lisa and Katie also get up from the audience and go towards a section of audience chairs.

Lisa, Katie, and the actors simultaneously start five small-group discussions. They begin by saying something like this:

"Before we get to the final section of the performance, we'd like to take about five minutes and talk together. How many of you know Lisa or Katie?" (Usually, a few people raise their hands.) "Well, as you all may know, Lisa and Katie would ask people four questions when they visited the Miltons. The questions were: How did you get to Milton? If there

was one thing you could change about the world, what would it be? What is your advice for future generations? Why do you think we are here on this earth? So, we'd like to take a moment to ask you all to answer one of these questions."

Each group leader chooses one of the questions and holds a brief discussion with the small group. After a few minutes, a tone sounds, and the group leader says, "Thanks so much. We're going to finish the show now."

Katie and Lisa sit back down and the actors stand between the banks of seats. The sky screens are illuminated, and the floating clouds fill the space.

2

And then you find out the firemen actually only break even on the stew, really they just make it as a community | event

    1 | And then you wish that everyone could have the experience you are having, sitting down with people who are so different from | you

        3 | And then you walk into High Street Baptist and see Miss Cleota in her beautiful | hat

           1 | You wish you could bring all five Miltons into one room.

3

And then you find out the drive-through is actually meant for people on | horseback

    2 | And then you find out the man sitting in front of you is the one you heard about, the one who was the crossing guard for | forty-five years

        1 | And then you turn the corner and see the breakfast Wilma has laid out for you, with boudin and crawfish | quiche

          2 | And then you look up, up and see all the gears that make the clock tower | work

3 | And you look down and see a tire decorated with flowers on the gravestone, and you know this must be Miss Patsy's dad's | grave.

1 | And then her husband tells you about how she
became one of the first female   **3**

Black female   **1**

Baptist preachers
in the area.

2
And then you realize her description of "God speaking to her" sounds a lot like you getting artistic
inspiration for your | plays

3 | And then Mr. Chavez points out the window and says "Why do you think that
tree is here on this | earth?"

1 | And then the door opens and two women come in
laughing about the possum they had to shoot in their yard
the night | before

3 | And then you open the front door and see
everyone who lives on the block decked out in
St. Patrick's Day | hats

2 | And then you find out he
makes earrings because he
used to tie fishing lures, and
one day his wife said wow,
those are | pretty

1 | And then you wish you could go on and on and list all of the doors you opened in
Milton, North Carolina that revealed something surprising, something that woke up
your | imagination

3 | And then you walk into the Chinese Restaurant and sit down with Little Joe, a
Country Western singer from the Umatilla | tribe

2 | But you know that if you started on that
list, the show you are writing would be
twelve | hours long

1 | And you open the door to
First Parish Unitarian and there's
a different church using the space:
they are Haitian and their service
is in | French

3 | And you walk into a bar and see the "Milton Hall of Fame," a wall filled with plaques honoring local sports | heroes

      2 | And then you walk into a middle school class and see the diversity of the town sitting right there in front of you   **3**

            And you climb the steep stairs at the top of the weather observatory and emerge out onto a roof under a cloudy sky, where Jim, your videographer, is standing by a video recorder pointed at the sky. He's been filming the sky for about 18 hours now, capturing footage to use in the performance you are making called *MILTON*.

The room darkens as the sky screens flicker to life once more: a cloudy day this time. Massachusetts sky after a storm, with the sun trying to break through.

1

It's 5am, and you hear footsteps behind you, and you realize it must be Observer Bob, the man you heard about yesterday, who shows up here every morning to look out onto the horizon and determine the visibility for the day and call it in to the weather stations   **3**

            A process which is way more subjective than you would think

      1

      Because it's determined by landmarks he can see or not see. And the clouds are moving, and he starts telling you about them—

1 places his hand on a speaker and we hear Observer Bob's actual voice—an older man with a thick Boston accent. Soon, 3 begins to sing with 1 and 2 humming.

OBSERVER BOB: See them drifting over the summit? There they are right there. See it blowing by there? That's stratus.

KATIE: Wow look how it's opening up right there.

OBSERVER BOB: It's opening up. The sun is breaking through. They're actually seeing the sun shining through and that's why we're seeing the bright sky right here. Anytime now! You're going to see the disc. So I hope you're ready with your cameras. Or whatever you're going to paint it. Photograph it?

KATIE: Yep. With that video camera.

OBSERVER BOB: That's Southwest there. That's a mile. And over here—there's a pond that's a mile and a half. You can't see it. There's a pond right there! That's a mile. Do you see it over there?

KATIE: Yeah yeah I see it!

OBSERVER BOB: That's a mile. That's Houghton's Pond. And Ponca Park is over here. But you can't see it at a mile and a half. So visibility is now all the way from East Southeast—actually East to Southwest—one mile . . .

There it is! There's your disc! See that come in now? Sun disc visible. It's occasionally visible

3

Visibility is Low today—

I can barely see my hand.

We call this low visibility.

When you can see as far as Houghton's Pond—

That means visibility is better.

This is a very typical fog.

Clouds . . . see them drifting over the summit!

There they are right there—
See them blowing by there?

because it's disappeared now . . . Back again.

KATIE: Hey Jim come on up! The sun disc is showing up.

OBSERVER BOB: The sun disc is now visible. This is a very typical fog. It's increasing over here now . . .

Anytime now they're going to appear . . .

So get ready with your cameras or whatever.

You have to be ready—

You have to be patient—

And it will make itself visible.

Oh it's there, over there somewhere . . .

See that faint glow?

Get ready . . .

Hmm.

The actors turn off the lamps and the sky screens glow for one more brief moment before settling.

END of PLAY

the process

meeting the miltons

We would first "meet" a Milton as a dot on a map displayed on one of our laptops. If the Milton had a town website, we'd go there to look at photos and read lists of organizations. Then comes the thrill of landing physically in a Milton: a road that used to be just a curvy line on a computer screen would wind through a distinct landscape of houses, businesses, green spaces. Then we'd walk into, say, the library. Then we'd sit down with an actual person who runs adult programs, and then that person would know another person we really should meet, and suddenly . . . we'd find ourselves sharing French fries with members of the senior bowling league in Milton, WI (p.36)*, or picking grapes in Milton-Freewater, OR with a Mexican immigrant crew (p.47), or crawling out onto the roof of a weather observatory in Milton, MA (p.63) to meet the man who has been recording weather visibility by hand every day for the past fifty years (p.23) .

In the beginning, we thought it was important to share the scope and complexity of our project immediately upon meeting folks. But we quickly learned that announcing ourselves as "performance-makers interested in exploring questions about our country" or "experimental theater artists doing a community-responsive project" usually just confused people. Eventually we started telling people we were writing a play about their town. It wasn't the whole story, but it was a clear entry point (although we would still get introduced as "the girls doing the movie" or "the girls writing the book").

We say "suddenly," but it took a lot of trial and error to figure out how to actually connect meaningfully with individual Miltonians.

Nov. 10, 2012: It is our second visit to Milton, MA. We have just finished walking through the public library, leaving hand-written notes next to people working at the upstairs tables: "When you're ready for a break, come down to the cafeteria and talk to two artists about your town!" We thought surely someone would be curious enough to come say hello. No one was. Instead, picture us: two polite-looking white women in their 40s sitting under a large "Who is Milton?" sign. People of all ages and races move through the cafeteria, glance at the sign, and give us a puzzled look, a sheepish smile, or ignore us completely.

We knew we wanted to meet and talk with people. We knew we wanted to fight stereotypes about the kind of person who lives in small towns. And we knew we wanted to find a way to access their interior lives, their deeply held beliefs, without seeming pushy or arousing suspicion.

PearlDamour performances deal with intellectual, existential topics. We don't make traditional "documentary theater," where, say, an actor embodies an actual person from the town. We were interested in conversations that would lead to a more associative, poetic, theatrical experience. We made lists of possible questions: What do you know about the day you were born? What makes you feel like home? What do you work the hardest for? Where does your wisdom lie?

We were eager to get to the "good stuff." We just weren't sure how.

> *Sept. 23, 2012: The pastor of the Unitarian Church in Milton, MA agrees to gather a group of six interested parishioners to stay after church and talk with us on our first visit. We buy snacks, go to the service, and then gather with the group in a small side room when it's done. After a brief intro and project description, we ask eagerly: "So, do you think you can ever truly know another person?" The question falls like a lead balloon: flat faces, instant mistrust. Were we members of some kind of cult? Or just loopy artists doing some touchy-feely project? One member of the group politely excuses herself. We blush and backpedal. "Well, how did you each get to Milton?" we ask instead . . . and little by little, the ice begins to break.*

---

* Throughout the following essays, page numbers refer to the moment in which a particular detail appears in the NC script.

connections

We made initial visits to the five Miltons within the first six months of the project. Certain features leapt to the surface:

- Four of the Miltons are either on the verge of disappearing or in the middle of an identity crisis because of the loss of a specific industry (p.48). We could feel the frustration of the residents, and the void left behind when industries collapsed—farming, auto manufacturing, paper and lumber mills.

- Many people we encountered are working more than one job—sometimes out of necessity, sometimes out of passion. The community development director also does equine massage. (p.45). The prison guard sells jewelry at craft fairs. The schoolteacher helps manage the family farm. The real estate agent bakes bread during the morning shift at the bakery. And so on.

- Hardly anyone wants to talk politics, especially in the smaller Miltons. But most people are eager to talk about their town and how it can be more livable. And a healthy handful of those people have the time and want to get their hands dirty and do something about it.

- All of the Miltons are at a critical moment around race and shifting demographics. And like the rest of the country, they needed healing and tools to talk about it. Many individuals seem ready and willing to start. It's getting into a group—especially a racially mixed group—that is hard.

- All of the Miltons are filled with empty buildings—many of them gorgeous—waiting to be filled with people and used by the community. Often the obstacle to filling them is paying for upkeep and maintaining insurance. Sometimes the obstacle is proposed developments that will change the nature of the building or the neighborhood.

- Artists are everywhere. They make soap and furniture and blankets out of brown cotton (p.33); they build parade floats and plant gardens and put together Adirondack chairs out of old water skis (p.21). Most often, the artists we met didn't identify or showcase themselves that way. In the larger Miltons, people were more ready to call themselves artists, to use that word and claim that identity—perhaps because there are organizations to support them or places to show their work.

- Bubbles are everywhere, keeping us in our comfort zones and away from people who are different or hold different views. These bubbles can be hidden, so much a part of our lives that we don't notice them: perhaps you have a big family, a vibrant church community, or a particular place where you always meet to socialize. Perhaps you have a lot of money so you never have to ask for help, or have no money so you are working nights and weekends with no time to connect with others.

- People have a real interest in mixing with others from different cultures/races. But often the folks we talked to didn't know where to begin, or had been burned or let down by previous efforts, or didn't have the time, training, or support to make the kind of conscious, sustained effort that reaching across lines of race and culture requires.

the people

So we're in Milton. How do we meet people?

In the smaller Miltons, it was pretty easy to get introduced around. People liked to take us under their wing. We quickly learned to schedule our trips only half full—the people we met on the first day of our visit almost always had ideas about people we should meet and places we should see; the rest of our schedule would fill up instantly. We learned how easily things can get done in a small town. In Milton, NC, it only takes about four minutes to get from one side of town to the other. Many people there were self-employed or retired, so someone like Joe Graves of the Thomas Day Society could say, "Oh you have to meet Twinkle! She's something else!" and within the hour we would be sitting at Twinkle's dining room table, eating chicken-salad shells and hearing stories about her great-great-grandmother, who was an African American midwife famous in the area. Joe Graves was one of our "connectors" in Milton, NC. We had several in each Milton.

Now we're in the room with a group of Miltonians. What next?

Our awkward first experiences taught us to keep it simple. Ask someone a straightforward question and then give them room to speak. People are complex. The "good stuff" will come. We tried out some starter questions, revised them, tried out some more and revised again. Finally we landed on four questions that we asked everyone we interviewed. Often folks were nervous when they sat down with us, so we developed a strategy of laying out all four questions first, to give people a chance to take them in.

May 27, 2013: Lisa and Katie sit in the tiny office of the head librarian at the library in Milton-Freewater, OR—a man known around town as "Library Bob." He has graying hair, a pet pig (p.22), and is probably in his late 60s. He has a passion for hosting "music nights" at the library (p.42), gathering people together to play records organized around a theme or decade.

KATIE: When we talk to people, we like to ask them four questions. Do you want to know what they are?

LIBRARY BOB: Yes, sure.

LISA: OK, great. The questions are: How did you get to Milton? If there were one thing you could change about the world, what would it be? What is your advice for future generations? And why do you think we are here on this earth?

Lisa, Katie and Library Bob all laugh. Pause. Expectant silence.

LIBRARY BOB: Wait. You want ME to answer those?!

KATIE: We do!

LIBRARY BOB: Okay, now tell them to me again . . .

The four questions led to exchanges that felt more like conversations than interviews. Our first question, "How did you get to Milton?" seemed basic but led to enticing stories about families being in the town for generations and how the town had changed, or about the job opportunities, losses, or loves that brought newcomers to settle there. The other three questions moved the conversation through personal opinion, foundational value, and life philosophy. Sometimes our talks were short—30 minutes—and sometimes they stretched to one or two hours, winding through topics we hadn't anticipated.

We had conversation after conversation. Each new person led us deeper, bit by bit, into the complexity of each town. We never knew how we were going to "use" this "material," because we weren't there just to gather information, make a product and move on. We were there to talk and listen, to exchange and connect.

We often left our visits exhilarated and overwhelmed. How to navigate the historical, political, and cultural complexity of these communities? And how to reflect and respect it in our performance?

ways we met miltonians

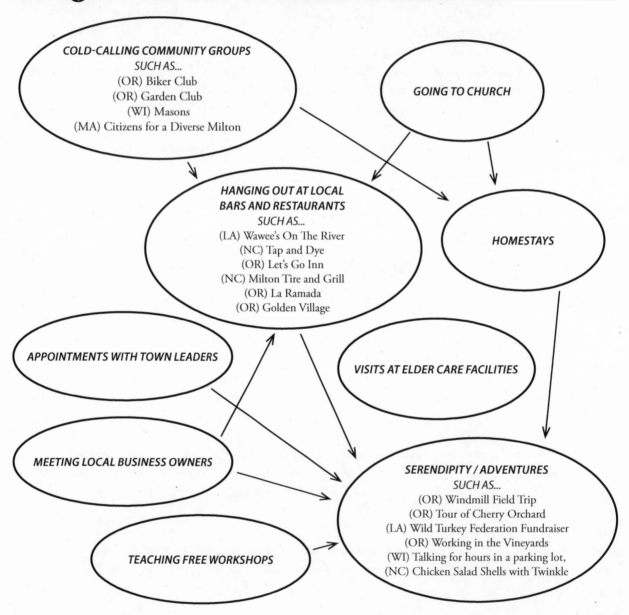

COLD-CALLING COMMUNITY GROUPS
SUCH AS...
(OR) Biker Club
(OR) Garden Club
(WI) Masons
(MA) Citizens for a Diverse Milton

GOING TO CHURCH

**HANGING OUT AT LOCAL
BARS AND RESTAURANTS**
SUCH AS...
(LA) Wawee's On The River
(NC) Tap and Dye
(OR) Let's Go Inn
(NC) Milton Tire and Grill
(OR) La Ramada
(OR) Golden Village

HOMESTAYS

APPOINTMENTS WITH TOWN LEADERS

VISITS AT ELDER CARE FACILITIES

MEETING LOCAL BUSINESS OWNERS

SERENDIPITY / ADVENTURES
SUCH AS...
(OR) Windmill Field Trip
(OR) Tour of Cherry Orchard
(LA) Wild Turkey Federation Fundraiser
(OR) Working in the Vineyards
(WI) Talking for hours in a parking lot,
(NC) Chicken Salad Shells with Twinkle

TEACHING FREE WORKSHOPS

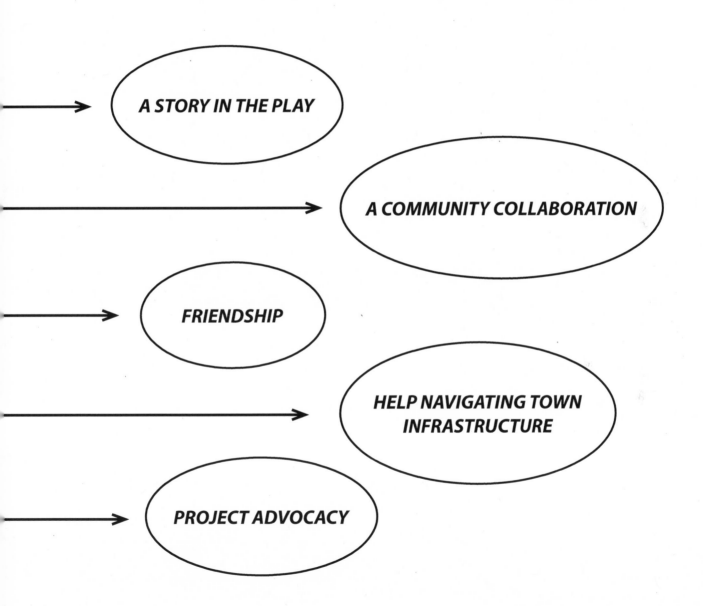

community engagement

June 21, 2014: 3pm, Milton, NC, on the day of the first annual Milton Street Fair. Other Miltonians have just shared their stories about the town in PearlDamour's Elder Story Circle. Outside the defunct gas station, people stand in line in front of a white pop-up tent for fish sandwiches and sno-cones from the High Street Baptist Fish Fry, and for tomatoes, cantaloupe, and carrots from Donald Lea's vegetable stand. On the other side of the street is Milton Presbyterian Church, where local actor Fred Motley is performing his piece on Thomas Day, a famous African American cabinet-maker from Milton in the 1800s. The antique stores are all open, the sidewalks in front of them covered with whimsical artworks created this morning in the sidewalk art contest. Outside the art gallery, Shirley Cadmus has a crowd gathered as she demonstrates how to make a "face vase" on her potter's wheel. Herman Joubert, a local resident, plays James Taylor on his guitar. A few blocks up in the parking lot of the Tap and Dye (a tie dye shop and bar), a local band plays rock music, and a new resident of Milton is putting on a blacksmithing demonstration. Cleota Jeffries, a 90-year-old Milton native, is sitting next to her relatives who are helping with the Fish Fry: "Milton is in bloom," she says.

Making things with Miltonians was key to building relationships with individuals, organizations, and town governments. There was a chicken-and-egg quality we liked: were the community projects context for the performance, or was the performance context for the projects?

Yes and Yes.

We describe our project as a performance and community engagement experiment. Calling it an experiment helped us acknowledge that we were new to this kind of community-based work, and helped us flow through the many unknowns in trying to connect with five towns. It also allowed us to bring together a variety of different community-based theories and techniques.

We consulted Alternate Roots, a network of socially engaged artists in the Southeast United States, about strategies for introducing ourselves to these towns, and eventually hired Ashley Sparks to work with us as our engagement strategist. Ashley had attended the Cornerstone Institute at Cornerstone Theater in Los Angeles during Bill Rauch's tenure as Artistic Director, and subsequently worked

78

for them handling community partnerships. She also produced the Network of Ensemble Theatres Micro-Fests in four cities across the country, and had a wealth of experience facilitating community conversations. She was a vital member of our team—an in-house, on-the-ground advisor, especially in North Carolina and Oregon.

We were also inspired by Jo Carson's work on the biology of community storytelling, and relied heavily on the structure and ethos of "Story Circles," a technique commonly used today but first developed by John O'Neal of the Free Southern Theater and Junebug Productions in the late 1960s.

We decided early on that we wanted to bring our aesthetic to these towns, using trained actors who could handle poetic language and a challenging vocal score. Locals participated through interviews and opening acts. This was fantastic, but we still wanted deeper artistic collaborations with local residents in each Milton. We started asking locals about how our skills could be useful to them. What were some town priorities? How were people addressing those issues? Were there sticking points? Could art help?

Here's how it happened in Milton, NC.

In January 2013, about six months before the show was scheduled to go up, we held a meeting at the Thomas Day House—a building in Milton's tiny downtown which serves as a museum for the work of a free Black cabinet-maker who worked in Milton in the mid-1800s, and also as a town hall where people can pay their water bills. We'd invited people to come learn more about our show and bring ideas for a local art collaboration—something we could make together. About 20 people attended, including key connectors from both the Black and white communities. We thought they'd suggest something like a community potluck dinner. And then Shirley Cadmus, who runs the Milton Studio Art Gallery, raised her hand. "I'd like to propose a Guild Day, where artists can do demonstrations and sell their artwork." There was an immediate enthusiastic response. Within an hour Shirley's idea grew into what would become the First Annual Milton Street Fair.

Our community collaborations began differently in each Milton, and each grew organically. But their starting points were always the needs and interests of that particular community.

In each town, we felt varying degrees of interest/eagerness to use art and conversation to bring the town's challenges into the open. Each town generated ambitious new ideas to try out. And like many first-time projects, there were aspects that fell away and discoveries made for the future. It was important to us that there would be a next try—that these activities and programs could continue to grow after our show was over.

We engaged in three large-scale community collaborations:

- *Milton Street Fair in Milton, NC*
- *Talk Play Dream–Hablar Jugar Soñar in Milton-Freewater, OR*
- *Milton Reflecting in Milton, MA*

Expanded information about each project can be found in Appendix B: Community Projects.

long distance collaboration

Like any relationship, our connection to the Miltons required attention and care—even though we lived many miles from each town. During our visits, we were intentional about spending one-on-one time with our partners to catch up on personal life developments and town politics, and to re-articulate the developing goals for our partnership. Once we left, folks' lives moved quickly without us, and while we were thinking of them, they weren't necessarily thinking of us. Sometimes all it took was an occasional "hello" on the phone or over email to keep a connection alive until our next visit.

relationship building = audience building

Our collaborations with the community helped folks feel our presence. They deepened our relationships, guided our conversations, and contributed to the cultural landscape in each town. They also helped build our audience.

Much of the audience for our show was made up of people with whom we crossed paths or collaborated: parents who brought a child to a cloud-making workshop, or the woman who organized the parade for Cinco de Mayo, or the church group who hosted a dinner for us during our tech week.

And then there were friends of people we had worked with, and the people we met around town at the diner or the bowling alley (in Wisconsin); at the pizza place or the church service (in North Carolina); at the biker bar (in Louisiana); at the library or the elder care residence (in Massachusetts); at the shoe shop or the panadería (in Oregon) . . . and so on.

To fill out the rest of the audience, old-school methods and word-of-mouth worked best. We walked around and brought postcards to people's front doors. We passed out flyers to classes we visited and encouraged the students to invite their parents. In Milton, MA, where people are more used to going to the theater, personal testimony about our show got on the neighborhood Facebook feeds and we were packed. In Milton, NC, we went to churches and introduced ourselves, talked about what we were doing, and brought sign-up sheets so people could commit to coming to the play right then. We also put sign-up sheets in local venues—like the post office, library, or gas station.

Shows were free and there was no online ticketing, but in each Milton we had a toll-free number people could use to reserve tickets—this was important in rural communities where many residents had less access to the Internet, but also really helpful in a larger town like Milton, MA. We called back every single person who reserved a ticket and talked to them personally. This last personal connection made folks feel more comfortable and committed.

Aug. 9, 2013: Midway through the performance in the Women's Club in Milton, NC. One of our actors says their line: "In the pocket of the Carhartt Overalls are some handmade earrings made by the man wearing the Carhartt Overalls." About half the audience laughs and looks towards Taco, who is sitting in the front row, wearing his Carhartt overalls, probably with earrings in the pocket. The actors laugh, too: "Take a bow, Taco!" one of them says. Taco grins, stands, and bows deeply as the audience applauds.

dramaturgy of participation

Throughout the *MILTON* project, we challenged ourselves to talk to strangers and dive into new experiences. We regularly experienced the terror of crossing the street to talk to someone new—only to find a whole new world opening up to us when we took the risk. This rule of thumb became a structuring principle that flowed through our research, creative work, and eventually our show. We call it "the dramaturgy of participation."

> *Aug. 4, 2014: In Milton, NC, 90-year-old Jean Scott is often our host (p.19). One morning over coffee, Katie tells Ms. Scott that she has a 'female partner' who would be coming to Milton to see the show, and that they were happy to stay elsewhere if that would be better. Ms. Scott nods, unfazed. "That's just fine," she says in her slow, rich voice. "What you do is your business. You are both welcome here." The interaction opens up a conversation about her nephew, who is gay, and a wonderful story about photos of her in-laws—who were long dead, and who were not her favorite people—that she had kept up over her fireplace for years, all the way up until her husband's last sister passed away (p.22).*

Opening ourselves up to strangers/people who held different values than us helped us empathize with other Americans trying to connect across race and class. If it was scary and exhausting for us—eager, confident artists with a driving need to make our show—what must it be like for, say, a working class parent striving to make ends meet? Is it a privilege to reach outside one's comfort zone?

We worked to create a structure for our show that gently mirrored the fear, joy, and complexity of our evolving participation in these towns. Our performance started with simply saying hello. Before the actors began, we introduced ourselves as the creators, Katie and Lisa, and pointed to video projections coming to life on translucent screens—pieces of sky floating above the audience. We saved the sky over the city we were performing in for last, which always triggered a burst of applause. This introduction let the audience meet us and "claim" their sky, and it gave people who were new to theater some context for the play.

Soon after, the actors began speaking from seats in and among the audience. They began slowly, listing images—little "flashes" from all five Miltons. As the list sped up, the actors got up from their chairs and started handing out photos and artifacts from each town. The room came alive with activity, audience members passing pictures and objects, cheering or laughing when they recognized something from their town. We could sense the joy of people feeling seen, of wanting to see the pictures from other Miltons, and of working to keep up with the show while passing things around the room.

This activity created a bond between actors and audience, and between individual audience members, laying a foundation for where the show went later. In the "beliefs" sections of the play, we addressed issues of racism and employment inequity, and eventually assigned hot-button beliefs to different audience members ("you believe that abortion should be legal," "you believe in the right to life," "you believe that Black lives matter," "you believe that all lives matter"). The jovial activity from earlier in the play created a space for the audience to hold the rifts and tension of this section. Actors and audience became a temporary community in which it was safe to dig deeper together.

After the "beliefs" section, recorded voices of dozens of Miltonians filled the space, and the actors floated glowing miniature clouds among audience. This was a chance for the audience to breathe, listen, and reflect. Then—just as saying hello to Jean Scott at a tiny Methodist church service led to long conversations over coffee at the breakfast table—the interactive strategies of the performance led to group conversation: Katie, Lisa, and the three actors each walked over to a different section of audience seats and asked them to have a conversation with us for five minutes. We launched these by asking one of our four interview questions:

- *How did you get to Milton?*
- *If there was one thing you could change about the world, what would it be?*
- *What is your advice for future generations?*
- *Why do you think we are here on this earth?*

The dramaturgy of participation prepared the audience for this moment; we almost always felt the audience was eager to talk and connect. By the end of the show, we hoped that the audience—whether sitting in a circle in an old church or on a high school stage or in the basement library community room—truly realized they were IN THE ROOM (p.60) with people from different cultural backgrounds, of different races, who held different values and world views. We hoped our play provided a framework for holding this diversity with curiosity, and seeing it as an asset for their town.

How can people activate the dramaturgy of participation in their neighborhood, their town or city, their country? For us, it meant taking a deep breath, crossing the street, and discovering something about that fellow American "over there."

We often wondered: what if there were a paid position—a "Town Diplomat" or "Town Connector"—someone in charge of putting you in a room with people different from yourself?

connecting the five miltons

Having connected with other people within their town, we wanted audiences to zoom out and see their town as part of a constellation of other towns, all filled with complexities, idiosyncrasies, needs, and challenges.

Many of them were facing similar issues around economy and race—could connecting town leaders help solve problems? We put several "connecting projects" in motion, but didn't quite have the capacity to fully keep them going. Here is what we tried:

AMBASSADORS:

When we first produced the show in Milton, NC, we had enough funding to invite an ambassador from each of the other Miltons to come. They saw the show and had a brainstorming session to discuss the play and how it might work differently in their Milton. The ambassadors were:

> **Pat Latimore**, *Founding member of Citizens for a Diverse Milton, Milton, MA*
> **Sue and Doug Duhon**, *Longtime residents of Milton, LA*
> **Mike Watkins**, *Community Development Director, Milton-Freewater, OR*
> **Brett Frazier**, *Mayor, Milton, WI*

The ambassadors were in Milton, NC for a quick two days. The town council held a celebratory reception toasting their arrival right before our show, and then everyone headed over to watch. The ambassadors were part of a post-show talk-back that night, discussing ways in which the show spoke to "their" Miltons. At a brunch the next day, we discussed challenges shared by each of the Miltons and how the play and related arts events could help address them. Having the ambassadors in town helped make the other Miltons "real" to the locals in Milton, NC, and also boosted town pride—it was great to see the ambassadors fall in love with this tiny Milton and buzz with excitement about its charm and potential.

> *Aug. 9, 2014: After the show, we hold an informal hangout at the Milton Tap and Dye—a tie dye shop and bar/music venue. Our creative team, the Milton ambassadors, and locals are all hanging out, drinking cold beer and talking about the show. We look over and see Pat Latimore,*

a cosmopolitan African American lawyer and activist from Milton, MA, two-stepping with Taco, a white prison security officer from Milton, NC, who has a side business making earrings out of fishing lures. City Milton and Country Milton, coming together on the dance floor!

We loved the ambassador visit so much. When we produced the show in Oregon and Massachusetts, our budget grew bigger, but so did the number of local arts collaborations, and we couldn't stretch the money and our time enough to make it happen in the other two towns.

GIFT EXCHANGES:

When we were hosted by someone in one Milton, we asked them to send us away with something that represented their town or their family—something we could give away. Then, when we stayed with someone in another Milton, we gifted them that thing, telling them about the person who gave it to us. It was a low-key and satisfying way to make a personal connection happen between strangers. (Sometimes we did this with small items we picked up ourselves in the Miltons—library bookmarks, or coasters from restaurants, and it worked just as well.)

PERSONAL VISITS:

Of course many locals expressed a desire to visit the other Miltons. We know it happened at least once: after *MILTON* premiered in Oregon, Jean Ann Mitchell, who organized the pop-up art galleries in Milton-Freewater, went to visit Shirley Cadmus, who runs the Studio Art Gallery in Milton, NC. The two were able to compare notes on the *MILTON* project, and discuss the joys and challenges of being a working artist in a small town. We also got a note from a Milton, MA couple who had been following the project and stopped in to the Milton Tire and Grill in North Carolina for a breakfast and a visit during a road trip.

talking about race

MILTON-FREEWATER, OR
Population: 7,027
White: 48%
Hispanic or Latinx: 49.3%
American Indian or Alaska Native: 3.1%
Two or More Races: 2.4%

MILTON, LA
Population: 2,460
White: 97.2%
African American: 2.8%

MILTON, MA
Population: 27,575
White: 71.9%
African American: 15%
Asian: 6.6%
Hispanic or Latinx: 4%
Two or More Races: 3.1%

MILTON, WI
Population: 5,581
White: 92.8%
African American: 1.9%
Hispanic or Latinx: 3.6%
Two or More Races: 1.7%

MILTON, NC
Population: 250
White: 42.78%
African American: 57.22%

With the exception of Milton, WI, each of the Miltons were in the middle of their own unique moment of shifting demographics or perceptions about race. We had to face the fact that we— two outsiders coming in to make a play—weren't going to solve, or even greatly impact, the racial dynamics of each town. However, our play and process could participate in the ongoing conversation around it. Our job was to meet and listen to as many people as possible, include them in our process, and do our best to make them feel seen and welcome in our show.

---

* These statistics are drawn from the U.S. Census Bureau, except for Milton, LA (drawn from Louisiana demographics. com, as the town is not incorporated) and Milton, NC (drawn from areavibes.com, as census data only provides info on Caswell County, not Milton itself).

We're white women, so we could introduce ourselves to the white communities in each Milton with relative ease, flowing from, say, a conversation at a mostly white Unitarian Church to an impromptu driving tour of the town to a lunch of fried clams (p.24). Our white femaleness was mostly non-threatening to the white people we met and we could build trust quickly. Connecting with communities of color—whether African American in NC, LA, and MA, or Latinx in OR—required more trust-building.

> *Snapshot: Walking into the tidy, two-bedroom home of Cleota Jeffries, an 89-year-old African American woman in Milton, NC. She's tiny—less than five feet tall—and after inviting us in to sit on the couch, she perches on an armchair next to a framed photo of the Obama family (p.36). Sitting across from her is Nancy Hughes, also African American and in her late 80s (p.46). Both women have lived in Milton their entire lives. Cleota tells us about calling Harriet Brandon—the white mayor of Milton—after she received our voicemail and our handwritten note. "I needed to make sure you weren't the flim flam man," she tells us. She invited Nancy so she would not have to meet us alone.*

We were in constant conversation with ourselves about our privilege. As part of the "educated artist" class we had a lot of freedom: Katie was on a graduate school fellowship when the *MILTON* project began, and Lisa had recently received a couple of playwriting awards that gave her freedom to travel and work on projects like this one without worrying about money. Our whiteness gave us access to longstanding white networks of white money and white trust. And though it took time to build trust with communities of color, we didn't really question our right to walk into an African American church or the Mexican housing project, or to get a drink at a dive bar where all the working class white guys hung out. Feeling comfortable walking into unfamiliar spaces or knocking on a stranger's door is one of the privileges of our whiteness.

What seemed to be a simple nut to crack—these diverse ethnic and religious groups are living just blocks away from each other! And so many of them are interested in coming together!—always proved more complicated. Finding points of connection—like conversations about family—helped break the ice. Opening up about parts of us that some locals might find exotic—like Katie's Jewishness, or Lisa's New Orleans-ness, also helped. Continuing to show up, trip after trip, was key.

Attendance by people of color was always lower than we had hoped at our shows and show-related events. We often felt like failures. And just as often, locals would tell us that even with the relatively low turnout it was a success, and the first time anything like this had happened in their town.

Here are some stories of our successes and failures.

MILTON, NORTH CAROLINA—A COMMUNITY SING AND A SCHEDULING MISHAP: After the success of the Street Fair in Milton, NC, we wanted to organize one more community event to bring people together and spread the word about our show. We brought the idea of a community sing to the Milton Presbyterian Church (a white congregation), and the High Street Baptist Church (a Black congregation). The churches decided we would start at Milton Presbyterian, where we would sing some of the songs traditionally sung at their church, with Mayor Harriet Brandon playing the organ, then progress to High Street Baptist, where one of our core collaborators, Shirley Wilson, would lead their choir in some songs. The PearlDamour team also prepared songs to share. The event was almost rained out—bad weather kept a lot of elders away—so attendance was small, particularly amongst the white community. But Mayor Brandon was there, and we all sang together and then attended a dinner cooked by the High Street congregation in their church basement.

Scheduling our show in Milton, NC was difficult because of our schedules and trying to work around some big auto races at a nearby racetrack (p.46). We consulted with the town council, which included a mix of Black and white residents, and decided on a date. A month or two later, we received a call from Shirley Wilson very upset, saying we had scheduled the show on the weekend of a huge church field trip, when many of the town's Black residents would be away. This may not sound like a huge deal, but in a town of 200, one field trip can take away half of your audience! We made it work—many of the people going on the field trip came to our final invited dress rehearsal, or to our Sunday night show—but it meant that our audience was relatively segregated, with a majority white audience on our formal show dates.

MILTON-FREEWATER AND THE BILINGUAL SCRIPT: The more time we spent in Milton-Freewater, the more we realized the town was filled with hundreds of Spanish-only speakers. Even so, we saw very few bilingual signs in civic buildings and in the library, and we felt a palpable divide: white people on the Milton side of town, Latinx people on the Freewater side. In order to truly reflect the town, we needed a bilingual script. We consulted with a local social worker about translation strategies—we knew we didn't want actors speaking English with translators on the side. We wound up using several techniques: actors translating for each other (sometimes Spanish into English, sometimes English into Spanish), actors using Spanglish, sometimes using our "sky screens" for written translation, and sometimes leaving the English or Spanish untranslated.

We brought in Carlos Vargas-Salgado, a Peruvian professor of Spanish and theater-maker from Whitman College, to help us adapt and translate the text. At times the script felt like a quirky Spanish-language lesson—our one white actor, an older man, played the part of a non-Spanish speaker to humorous effect. As we worked on the adaptation, we realized the dramaturgy of the play was shifting to include a layer about the difficulty of connecting when you can't understand your neighbor. Audience turnout for the performance was approximately 80% white, 20% Latinx. It was interesting to watch a mostly white audience respond to the bilingual script—to experience (for once) what it's like to not understand what's being said around you, and to be faced with the reality that they lived in a truly bilingual town.

MILTON, LA—IT'S ALWAYS BEEN THIS WAY: Milton, LA: The Catholic church stands at the center of Milton, LA, and we estimate about 80% of the people in town attend. We went a few times, and noticed that the white people sat in the front, and the Black people in the back. When we asked our white host about it, she shrugged and said, "Oh, it's just always been that way." A simple sentence, spoken by a woman we were very fond of, drove home the staying power of white supremacy.

MILTON, WI—THE UNDERGROUND RAILROAD: The Milton House Museum (p.49) was originally an inn built by Joseph Goodrich (p.35), who settled the town. It is now a museum devoted to the town's origins and history. The inn was a stop on the Underground Railroad—a picture of Sojourner Truth hangs on one wall, and visitors can go to the basement to see the secret tunnel and storeroom which were used to hide slaves making their way to freedom.

However, the Milton of today is 97% white. Longtime residents Jim and Linda Lyke told us that their kids never saw a single Black person, other than on TV, until they were in high school.

MILTON, MA—SHINING A LIGHT ON RACIAL PROFILING, AN INTERACTIVE MLK DAY: Each year in Milton, MA, the Interfaith Clergy Association (MICA) hosts a Martin Luther King Day celebration at a Black Baptist church. Schoolkids make art and write poems, choirs and dance groups perform, and there is always a keynote address. It's a great day, but many Miltonians point out it's basically the *only* day that the white and Black communities come together in Milton—and that even at this event, people who don't know each other rarely interact. We hatched a plan with MICA to use the keynote address slot to spark conversations between strangers. Katie and local partners led the activity, in which attendees were asked to turn to someone in the pew in front of or behind them and ask them a question designed to elicit personal stories about difference and stereotyping. It was pretty wonderful to look out and see Concord Baptist filled with pairs of people talking and sharing stories.

Our partners in Milton, MA talked to us at length about the importance of our play not backing down from speaking to the lived realities of Black Miltonians, particularly about the higher-than-average racial profiling that happens there. We referred to one incident in the dialogue of our play, and another in a section with recorded voices. Interestingly, the only pushback we got involved a reference to a swastika that was painted in a middle-school bathroom a month before our performance. A school staff member told the superintendent she felt our play "put Milton in a bad light."

> *May 17, 2017: It's about 25 minutes into the special performance for high school students in Milton, MA, and the 70 seats are filled with teens of many races. So far, they've been interested but wary—why are we at this play? Why is it so weird? In the section where the actors assign jobs to audience members, a white actor points to a Black student and says: "Your job is to recruit community members for local activities." An African American actor follows up: "Until you get questioned by the police for talking to another Black person in a parking lot." An electrifying silence,*

then the room erupts: snaps of agreement, "No she didn't!" From this point forward, the students are engrossed.

Throughout all these conversations, events, and exchanges, the key was continuing to show up. Continuing to flow. Continuing to plan the next event even if the last one did not go quite as we'd hoped. We weren't there as a massive theater company throwing around big money to make a show, we were just people—individual artists with curiosities and interests. In some cases, like in Milton, MA, our work around race resulted in community dialogues that are still in place today. However, most of the work lives on in ways that are less visible and more difficult to track.

Aug. 8, 2014: *The actors were in town for about five days before the show, and Joe Graves, a white man and one of our closest collaborators, hosted a lunch for us at his home. Joe was a history buff, and his farm was once a plantation, with a graveyard in the woods behind his house for the slaves owned by a previous farm owner's family. Over the course of the week, Joe got into a very personal conversation with Helga Davis, one of our actors, a Black woman of Nevisian descent, about the graveyard. Joe believed it was possible for an owner to have a good relationship to his slaves—to provide for them and respect them. For Helga, "ownership" was by definition oppressive and immoral. Over the course of the week we'd see Helga and Joe continuing their discussion— in the corner of the theatre, or the local bar, or the pizza place. Here is Helga's account of their conversation:*

On the day Joe hosted us for lunch, I asked whether or not there was a slave cemetery. He did not answer. A few days later, he said that he had heard my question, and that he was not ignoring me. There was, indeed, a slave cemetery and Joe asked if I would like to go and see it. Setting out on his tractor, we drove across the property and stopped in what just appeared to be woods. "Do you see them?" Joe asked. I kept looking and looking but there were no gravestones or points of demarkation I could decipher. Joe pointed to a stone, or, rather, what appeared to be an ordinary stone on the ground. As I looked closer, I began to see them. Everywhere. Stones and small rounded mounds of earth which held the bodies of my ancestors, the very foundation of our Nation. Joe bent down and picked an herb from the forrest floor and told me to chew it. It was bitter. Pipsissewa. I wanted so much to remember its name, this bitterness, first used by Native peoples to aid them during periods of hunger. I placed flowers near one of the stones and said, "Thank you." Joe told me that he was going to be buried in the slave cemetery. I found this disturbing and ironic. But he explained that knowing he was buried on that land guaranteed its remaining intact, thus leaving the slave graves intact. "No one would dare dig up the bones of a white man on this land."

very basic advice

Much of this we learned the hard way.

- *ASK:* Check in with your community partners about all your scheduling decisions: site visits, show dates, gatherings. They have a lot of information that you don't about the ebb and flow of the community, and they will know whether it's a good time or not. They can advise you on the best times for you to come to town in order to achieve your goals.

- *FOLLOW:* Follow the lead of your community partners. You might have a great idea about an event or collaboration you want to activate—but is it something the town cares about and wants? Find out what's important to them, and let the engagement grow from there.

- *IT'S NOT NECESSARILY A SHORTCUT TO DO IT YOURSELF:* It is tempting to sit down and write the grant yourself in the voice of your co-applicant. The town of Milton-Freewater asked us to do so with the NEA Our Town Grant. They said, "Sure! If you write it we're up for it!" But even if you show your co-applicant the draft, they aren't artists or producers and they may not realize how much work they will be asked to do, should they get the grant. Small towns have small infrastructures, so it is important to take the time to have some real conversations about capacity and priorities, and write the grant TOGETHER. The application may seem less ambitious on the surface, but will lead to more success and less stress.

- *LEAVE SPACE IN YOUR DAYS:* At first, when we planned site visits, we wanted to make good use of our time by filling every day up with appointments. We quickly learned to leave big chunks of space in our schedule to allow for spur-of-the-moment offers, chance encounters, left-turns, and tangents. Having a few anchor events in a day was plenty, and left us time to recuperate and recharge.

- *IN SMALL TOWNS, CONSIDER WORD-OF-MOUTH AND NON-INTERNET BASED ADVERTISING:* Not that you shouldn't advertise online, but sometimes word-of-mouth, gas station billboards, and posters work just as well, if not better. Examples: in Milton, NC, we stuffed the water bills with flyers, used "rack cards" at local establishments, spread the word through churches, and put up a roadside LED sign. In Milton, MA, we set up a recurring show on local access TV, and talked the project up at town events and Selectmen meetings. in addition to putting the word out through the local newspaper and neighborhood Facebook groups.

- **LISTEN WITH PRESENCE:** Try not to control the conversation to "get what you're after"—you'll end up with richer, more satisfying, and surprising exchanges when you leave space. We tried to shift our perspective from "conducting an interview" to "having a conversation."

- **HOSPITALITY AND GIFTS:** Bringing something from your own home to share—food, souvenirs—is a great way to spark appreciation, laying the groundwork for relationship-building. We often would ask hosts in one Milton to give us something that we could gift to hosts in another Milton. Sharing meals built affiliation with community partners, deepening our understanding of each other.

- **NOT THERE TO FIX THINGS:** You are a theater artist, not a savior. A collaborator, not a social worker. The ways you and your project can inspire a town should be based on the town's interests, not yours. You may think you know a town well because of the intensity of your experiences and closeness you feel to your new friends—but you are viewing it through a small, curated window. You have a lot to offer, but you are there to learn, respond, and engage—not to solve something you perceive as a problem.

- **BE TRANSPARENT:** The *MILTON* project was grounded in curiosity and deep, active listening. As an outsider, it requires time to build trust with the people you'd like to invite into a creative encounter. Our process was intimate and personal. We were transparent about our own lives and project goals with the Miltonians we met, just as we asked them to be transparent with us. It felt like an important risk to take as we sought honest, common ground in order to build something together.

Snapshot: About a month before the Milton, NC Street Fair, while PearlDamour is in town for a short visit, we hear that Harriet Brandon, a town elder and the mayor of Milton at the time, has stopped coming to planning meetings. We stop by her house to ask her why. She tells us the "young people" who are planning the fair "don't care what us old-timers think!" We ask for her opinions and ideas. Harriet tells us she has the town's very first fire truck (p.21)—a contraption meant to be pulled by horse and buggy—in her garage, and she thought it would be wonderful in the parade. She shows it to us—a gorgeous little wooden cart with a hose attachment, complete with an old-fashioned siren that sounds by turning a crank! We go to the organizers and bring up Harriet's idea. They agree the fire truck would be a great addition, and the antique fire truck winds up leading the parade that day. We find ourselves in this position quite a bit in the Miltons, almost accidentally bridging the divide between old and young, liberal and conservative.

where we are now

Spending five years on this project put us in contact with this country and a handful of individuals in ways that changed us all in small and big ways. We are impacted by these changes and our newly expanded awareness every day.

We are still in touch with many of our collaborators and conversation partners from each of the five Miltons, mainly through email and Facebook. Occasionally we or they will reach out with a question, to share an opportunity, or ask for some specific advice. Many of our collaborations in each town continue to play out in different ways; these are detailed in Appendix B: Community Projects.

As of this book's publication, we have yet to complete the performance circuit in Milton, Louisiana and Milton, Wisconsin. At the moment we don't have the capacity to raise the money or spend the time needed to bring the project to full fruition there, but we do want to have a closing event in each Milton: something to say thank you, and to let the people who invested their time and interest in us and the project know how their Milton worked its way into the whole.

An archive of the project is available at
www.skyovermilton.com

appendices

a: script comparisons

We have included three short excerpts from the Milton-Freewater, OR and Milton, MA scripts on facing pages. The Milton-Freewater, OR text appears on the light gray left-hand page. The Milton, MA text appears on the darker gray right-hand page. The page numbers at the top of each section refer you to the corresponding page in the Milton, NC script.

3

Sometimes cruzas por | una puerta de iglesia.

       2 | you go in through a church door.

3

Sometimes cruzas por | la puerta lateral cerca de la cochera.

       2 | you go in through the side door near the carport.

2

Sometimes atraviesas la puerta de un gimnasio donde jugó Kareem Abdul Jabbar cuando el gimnasio pertenecía al Colegio Milton y los Milwaukee Bucks lo utilizaron como su campo de entrenamiento.

3

. . . the door of a gymnasium

. . . played when the gym belonged to Milton College and the Milwaukee Bucks used it for their training camp.

1

A veces | you go in through the door of the library.

    2 | la puerta de la biblioteca.

1

A veces | you go in through the door of the dentists office after hours

    3 | la puerta del consultorio dental fuera de horas

1

and sit down with | the dentist Norm Saager

    3 | y sentarse con el dentista Norm Saager

2

Sometimes you go in through a church door.

1

Sometimes you go in through the side door near the carport.

3

Sometimes you go in through the door of a gymnasium where Kareem Abdul Jabbar played when the gym belonged to Milton College and the Milwaukee Bucks used it for their training camp.

2

A veces usted va a través de una puerta de la biblioteca.

1

Sometimes you go in through the door of a middle school.

3

Sometimes after a Martin Luther King Day service, you go in the door of a second floor apartment on Blue Hill Avenue right next to the church. The apartment belongs to Ron Bell, and he hands you a plate of sweet ham with pineapple, greens, and mac and cheese, cooked for the party by his friend Angie. ESPN is on the TV, the new Ta-Nehisi Coates book is on the shelf, there are Christmas carols coming from the stereo, and the tree is still up in the corner.

2

Sometimes you wonder if people would be opening their doors to you so readily if you weren't two nice looking white women.

1

to hear | about the different ways the town is trying to grow.

     3 | oír hablar de las diferentes formas en que la ciudad está tratando de crecer

1

Sometimes you wonder—

3

A veces te preguntas

1

If people would be opening their doors to you so readily

3

si la gente te estaría abriendo sus puertas tan fácilmente

1

if you weren't two nice looking white women.

3

si ustedes no fueran dos simpáticas mujeres blancas.

2

No abriría mi puerta a dos mujeres blancas

1

You wouldn't open your door?

Interruption: all lean in.

3
Actually, I meant to say this before—I wouldn't open my door.

2
If they knocked on it?

3
No. I'm not comfortable with that.

1
Yeah but you're an introvert.

3
Well their being 'white women' doesn't help.

1 & 2
Right.

3
Just wanted to put that out there.

1 & 2
OK | . . . But you'd like the cookies, though right?
   3 | The cookies are a nice touch.

2
No.

1
Even if they had cookies?   **3**
                              ¿Ni siquiera si traen galletas?

2
¡No! ¡Quién sabe lo que quieran de mí!

3 grabs Katie's face, squeezes cheeks.

3
¡Pero mira esta, se ve tan dulce! ¡No mata una mosca!

2
Lo siento. They can call me on my cell.

1
But you probably wouldn't answer.

The three look at each other. Maybe 3 gives a look or says, "You know he's right . . ."
to 2. Then 2 dives in, moving things forward.

All settle back into seats and continue.

1

Say it in English!

> *3 turns to an audience member.*

2

Crees en aparecidos.

1

You believe people should pull themselves up by their bootstraps.

3

You believe someone should sell bootstraps.

2

You believe someone should give away bootstraps for free,

1

You believe that the world is a scarier place now than it was 50 years ago.

2

Say it in Spanish.

1

You believe the world is more free than it was 50 years ago.

3

You believe in freedom of speech.

3
You believe in ghosts. **1**
                        You're squeaking at me. **3**
                                                It's like you're living in some utopia.

2
You believe in gun control **1**
                            You believe in some gun control **3**
                                                            You believe in the right to bear
arms **2**
      I have bare arms **3**
                        Really?

1
You believe it's important to spread joy.

2
You believe that everyone's on the earth to be part of one big puzzle that adds up to you're not exactly
sure what

3
You believe you should lock your doors.

2
You believe if you can help somebody, you should help them.

3
You believe that the world is a scarier place now than it was 50 years ago.

1

You believe that people should just shut up and be grateful.

2

Crees que los inmigrantes ilegales mexicanos están chupándose los recursos de nuestro país.

3

Crees que los inmigrantes ilegales mexicanos están haciendo los trabajos que la gente blanca simplemente ya no quiere hacer.

2

Crees que la gente blanca son simplemente codiciosos.

1

I can't understand you!

2

¡No te puedo entender!

3

You believe that we live in a big country that was built for people to live side by side, and live out many points of view.   **1**

                    But you don't want to be in the room with all of them.

3

Crees que vivimos en un país grande que fue construido para la gente a vivir al lado del otro, y vivir muchos puntos de vista.   **2**

                    Pero usted no sabe cómo estar en la habitación con todos ellos.

1

You believe the world is more free than it was 50 years ago.

3

That is such a selective assessment! How privileged can you get!?

2

It's true that we may just be reifying the rhetoric by giving voice to the—

1

Re-what-ing Ms. Academic?

2

(to 1) What's wrong with being an academic?

1

You think the intellectual elite is a TINY group of self-absorbed hypocrites who are completely out of touch with real America.

3

"Real America!"

2

I am not out of touch!

1

"Real America" means freedom of thought. Freedom of Speech!

3

You believe that we live in a big country that was built for people to live side by side, and live out many points of view.   **1**

But you are afraid to be in the room with all of them.

3

Crees que vivimos en un país grande que fue construido para la gente a vivir al lado del otro, y vivir muchos puntos de vista.   **2**

Pero usted no tiene tiempo para estar en la habitación con todos ellos.

1

I don't understand you.

2

Estoy cansado de la tradùcción.

No te entiendo.

Habla mi idioma.

¿Por qué no aprendes mi idioma?

Me necesitas.

No me entiendes.

Realmente no me miras.

Miras lo que quieres mirar.

1

I don't understand you.

Speak my language.

Why won't you learn my language?

You need me.

You don't understand me.

You don't really see me.

You see what you want to see.

3

Free if you have the PRIVILEGE to think and speak!

2

"Real America" was built on the belief that kidnapping and enslaving | an entire people was OK!

1 | Yes! It's really complex!

3

YES! Let's get complex! *(to everyone)* You believe that the prison industry—YES INDUSTRY— and the school-to-prison pipeline are the NEW slavery, and the only way to end it is a PROFOUND SHIFT IN POWER. But the dominant white bloc is pretty happy with the power they have, so that shift won't happen for another 250 years!

1

So then let's take action! *(pointing to someone else—not using clipboard, this is your own belief)* You believe that each day is an opportunity to start anew! This country is about growth!

1

(to 3) Yes! I am seeing that! Why do I feel defensive right now?

3

Because you don't understand me!

1

But I can learn about the experiences you have! I can CHOOSE to LEARN!

2

You believe that we live in a big country that was built for people to live side by side and live out many points of view.

2
Aprende mi idioma.

1
Learn my language.

    A stalemate.

3
¿Cómo sería ser como para estar en la habitación con todos ellos ?

1
Que?

2
What it would be like to be in the room with all of them?

1
To be | in the room with all of them.
    2 | Para estar en la habitacióncon todos ellos.

3
Para estar en la | habitación.
       1 | To be | in the room.
           2 | Para estar en la habitación.

1

You believe that we live in a big country that was built for people to live side by side and live out many choices.

3

You believe that we live in a big country that was built for people to live side by side, and live out different realities.

2

You believe that we live in a big country that is being built by many people.

3

But you don't know *how* | to be in the room with all of them

               2 | And you wonder what it would be *like* | to be in the room

                             3 | To be | in the room

                                 1 | with all of them.

2

To be in | the room

        3 | To welcome them | in . . .

                1 & 2 | To be in the room . . .

In this section, translations in Spanish or English appear and disappear on the screens in time with the actors speaking. Some screens simply flash the words "And then . . ." or "Y luego . . ."

2
Y luego te enteras que drive-through is actually meant for
people on | horseback.

    1 | Y luego caminas hasta la Iglesia Amor and see Isabel leading the service with her strong | voice.

        3 | And then the 7th grader tells you her sonido favorito es el viento atravesando la alfalfa en la mañana—because she goes out to take care of the pigs and the cows before | school.

            1 | Y levantas la vista y ves Rick Rambo teetering on top of an extension ladder raspando la pintura vieja de un costado del edificio with the Heritage Club kids so they can repaint it for Make A Difference | Day.

                2 | Y miras abajo y ves el periódico de Elks Club, con las fotos de la Celebration de la Vida a de Harvey Sample, and remember hanging out with Harvey and Jan in the kitchen, hearing the strange and wonderful story of how they | met.

                    3 | Y entonces te das cuenta que su descripción de "Dios le habla a ella" sounds a lot like you getting artistic inspiration for one of your | plays.

                        2 | And then Fil Chavez points out the library window and says "¿Por qué

3
And then you find out the drive-through is actually meant for
people on | horseback.

> **1** | And then you find out that the school that first reminded you of a mini-UN is having
> swastikas | graffitied in the bathroom.

>> **2** | And then you learn that one of the apartment blocks Mexican families live in
>> is still called | the Labor Camp.

>> **1** | And then the library says: yes come in.

> **3** | And then you find out the shoe stitcher loves his job because working alone is helpful
> for his | PTSD.

>> **2** | And then the young Latino man who returned to Milton after college looks at you
>> and says, "It's our turn."   **3**

>>> And then you find out he makes earrings because he used
>>> to tie fishing lures, and one day his wife said wow, those
>>> are | pretty . . .

>> **1** And then you look up, up and see all the gears that make the clock
>> tower | work.

>> **2** | And then her husband tells you about how she
>> became one of the first female   **3**

>>> Black female   **1**

>>> Baptist Preachers
>>> in the area.

2
And then you realize her description of "God speaking to her" sounds a lot like you getting artistic
inspiration for your | plays.

> **3** | And then Mr. Chavez points out the window and says "Why do you think that
> tree is here on this | earth?

>> **1** | And then you open the front door and see everyone who

crees que aquel árbol está aquí sobre esta | tierra?"

3 | And then you walk into Golden Village y te sientas con dos cantantes vaqueros, Coyote Joe—part Navajo—and Little Joe, who is | Yakima.

2 | And then you hear about how Mac Hi was built in 1922, y que este teatro fue llamado así por Jack Williams, quien presentó su "Maytime Medley" justo aquí en este | teatro.

1 | And then you get a text message that the School Bond passed

1 & 2
by a margin of 80 percent—!

3
por un margen del 80 por ciento—!

1
And you wish you could go on and on and list all the doors you opened in | Milton . . .

3 | Y entonces deseas que todo el mundo tuviera la experiencia que estás teniendo.

1
But you know if you started on that list the show would be 12 hours long!

2 & 3
Pero sabes que si comenzaste en esa lista ¡el espectáculo duraría 12 horas!

lives on the block decked out in St. Patrick's
Day | hats.
    3 | And then you wish you could go on and on and list
    all the doors you opened in Milton, Massachusetts

1
List all the people who woke up your imagination, who taught you something about living in
this country **3**
    But you know that if you started that list, the show you are writing would be
    twelve | hours long.
      2 | And you walk into the Selectmen's meeting intending to talk to just three
      people and realize instead you're being televised to the whole town.

1
And you open the door to First Parish Unitarian and there's a different church using the space:
they are Haitian and their service is in | French
        3 | And you sit down for a high school play and see people
        of every color and culture sitting there around you.

  1
And you jump to your feet to applaud the Black Cinderella and the Asian-American
Prince Charming, and the woman next to you turns to you grinning with tears in her
eyes. "You're watching history being made in Milton," she says.

b: community projects

THE NEED:
Milton's business district lines three blocks of Highway 57, and includes three restaurants, several antique and craft shops, a museum, and an art gallery. It's a busy road, but most often vehicles barrel through without stopping. There is also a lack of foot traffic—with no gas station, grocery store, library, or school, there just aren't a lot of reasons for people to come to town. It's hard on business and hard on morale. How to make people pay attention to Milton, its artists, and its businesses? How to make Milton a destination folks are excited about coming to?

DEVELOPING THE iDEA:
After an enthusiastic town meeting where residents expressed a desire to show off their town's art and history, the planning team began working on its vision: a weekend-long community event that brought vendors, craftspeople, musicians, tourists, and inspired residents together to enjoy and celebrate their town. PearlDamour acted as consultants, drawing on our years of theater producing and event planning, and contributed $400 towards marketing efforts. The local committee members designed "rack cards" that could be left in neighboring towns, created Street Fair T-shirts (wearable marketing!), and placed notices in local papers and radio shows. They recruited and organized vendors and participants, and raised the rest of their budget by gathering donations from local businesses acknowledged on a sign the day of the fair.

KEY PARTNERS (PEOPLE AND ORGANIZATIONS):

- The Milton Studio Art Gallery (p.46) was the de facto headquarters for the Street Fair, and sponsored many demos and activities. Owner Shirley Cadmus spearheaded the planning and designed the T-shirt and the rack cards.

- Hosanna Blanchard is a craftsperson and small business owner in Milton. She was a leader throughout the planning, and made sure there was a kids' area, including a petting zoo, for the fair. Her partner Kevin took on maintenance and custodial duties. Hosanna spearheaded the planning for the 2nd Annual Street Fair, and worked with us to write additional grants for funding.

- The Thomas Day Historical Society (p.35) hosted museum tours and sponsored a one-man performance about Thomas Day.

- High Street Baptist Church (p.34) handled the Fish Fry and ran the food court.

THE EVENT:

PearlDamour arrived several days before the fair to help with the final prep. There were all sorts of great activities planned, but the planning committee hadn't figured out to how to communicate to visitors when and where it was all taking place. So we drew a bird's-eye-view map of the business district with vendor locations marked, and created a schedule to be photocopied and placed on doors the next day.

The organizers wanted to have a parade to launch the fair. They didn't have time to decorate cars or build floats, so they used the town's antique fire truck and had someone carrying a flag lead the way. PearlDamour bought little yellow umbrellas, to match the yellow of the street fair T-shirts. We decorated them with paint pens and beads, New Orleans style, and had people carry them in the parade and throughout the rest of the day.

The street fair was thrilling. We'd visited Milton many times, and starting at about 11am the streets were more packed than we had ever seen them. PearlDamour set up a display showing off our play and the five Miltons. We taught a cloud-making workshop and hosted an elder story circle to capture town history. It was a great way to meet new people and spread the word. And throughout the day, we saw people carrying and spinning their street fair umbrellas—they added a great visual splash to the festivities and worked as a kind of celebratory glue, circulating throughout the fair.

Through PearlDamour's participation, our project became embedded in an ecosystem of arts and community. It was a mutually beneficial event for PearlDamour and the town, and as a result, residents began to feel more ownership of and familiarity with our *MILTON* project—they became our best marketers and advocates as the piece moved towards its premiere. Our audience developed through making something with the people who would eventually come see our show—most traditional marketing tools like print, radio, or TV ads felt flat and uninspired in this context. As we built the street fair with the town, the town's trust in us grew—which made it easier to move forward together.

FOLLOW UP / THE FUTURE:

We led an energized debrief session after the street fair and it was immediately clear that it should become an annual event. We made "plus/delta" lists with the planning team, assessing what had worked and where problems had popped up; we built a work list and calendar. Over the course of the year we had a few phone consultations and came in for one community planning session.

The 2016 street fair coincided with the run of our show in Milton-Freewater. To connect the two, we sent a colleague from Durham to Milton, NC to run a children's activity booth where kids wrote down their favorite ways to be creative on large raindrops, assembling them on a mural called "Milton Rains Down Creativity." There was a display about the entire *MILTON* project and its progress. As of 2019, the fair continues—with 2019 planned as an off-year so the organizers can reflect and regroup. Every year has included a live performance about the life of Thomas Day, either in the Women's Club or in the Presbyterian Church. The folks in Milton feel like the street fair has put Milton back on the map, at least for that one day each summer, and the positive impact of that day is felt throughout the whole year.

MILTON-FREEWATER, OR—TALK PLAY DREAM – HABLAR JUGAR SOÑAR

THE NEED:

The 7,000-person population of Milton-Freewater, OR is about 50-50 white/Latinx and the majority of adults are mono-lingual English or Spanish speakers. Many locals and city hall feel that the two communities need to come together for the city to thrive. In addition, local artists want to make themselves seen, and folks want more art events in town so they won't always have to drive to the larger, more cosmopolitan Walla Walla, Washington for their "culture fix." Our local partners wonder with us: what can be done to bring the two sides of town together and energize local cultural and community development efforts?

DEVELOPING THE IDEA:

To start, we looked around for events, organizations, and people that were already active in town, and asked how PearlDamour could work with them. One of our first partners was the Milton-Freewater Downtown Alliance (MFDA), a small, lively community development organization devoted to energizing Milton-Freewater's downtown. One of their yearly activities was a Cinco de Mayo Festival. Using the festival and our show as anchor events, we worked with the MFDA and other key partners to develop bilingual, family-friendly creative activities to happen throughout the year. We called the series "Talk Play Dream – Hablar Jugar Soñar." The events were designed to bring locals citizens together to "talk, play, and dream" about the future of the town.

KEY PARTNERS (PEOPLE AND ORGANIZATIONS):

- City of Milton-Freewater—We worked with the city government to write our first successful NEA Our Town Grant to support Talk Play Dream – Hablar Jugar Soñar. We developed our relationship by attending city council meetings and working closely with Mike Watkins, the Community Development Director.

- Milton-Freewater Downtown Alliance (MFDA) helped us understand the landscape of civic development in Milton-Freewater, and sponsored the annual Cinco de Mayo Festival, which they saw as an opportunity for the Latinx and white communities to come together to celebrate the town. We put some of our grant funding toward growing the festival through equipment and programming. Randy, who ran the MFDA at the time, was always up for a phone call or brainstorming session.

- Jean Ann Mitchell, Arts Portal Gallery—An artist with a vision of creating a permanent arts center downtown, Jean Ann launched the Arts Portal Gallery to turn empty storefronts into temporary galleries. The grants we wrote together provided equipment that would make room for live music and spoken-word performances in the gallery.

- Melissa Cunnington, McLoughlin High School Drama/Choir Teacher—Melissa invited us into her classroom to teach workshops and make short plays for Walla Walla's Day of the Dead Festival and Milton-Freewater's Cinco de Mayo Festivals.

- Mayra Osorio, The Heritage Club—The Heritage Club is a group of high school students committed to preserving and celebrating their Hispanic heritage. Mayra Osorio (also an active member of MFDA) was a steadfast partner throughout (p.40).

- Shakespeare Walla Walla—A professional theater company one town over, Shakespeare Walla Walla co-wrote some major grants with us, served as our 'on the ground partner' for several grant activities, particularly in the schools, and co-produced our production of *MILTON*.

- The Public Library—We held several events at the library, a place where the entire community (especially students) seemed to feel comfortable and welcome.

- The Frazier Farmstead Museum—We met Diane Biggs (p.60) who ran the Frazier Farmstead early on and interviewed her for the show. Later, the Farmstead hosted us for some of our community roundtables.

THE EVENTS:
Talk Play Dream – Hablar Jugar Soñar used existing places and events as points for creative programming that touched many folks—even if only once—in the eight months leading up to our play:

FALL:
- Creative workshops with high-school and middle-school classes.

- Day of the Dead Festival—Shakespeare Walla Walla worked with McLoughlin High School students to bring a silent tableau version of *Macbeth* to Shakespeare Walla Walla's Día de los Muertos celebration. The high school troupe travelled to nearby Walla Walla, which also has a growing Latinx population, and performed the play in full Día de los Muertos face paint alongside other abridged versions of Shakespeare's plays. We passed around photos of their performance during our *MILTON* show.

WINTER:
- Creative workshops with high-school and middle-school classes.
- Cloud-making workshop at library—We had a few bilingual speakers on hand to facilitate involvement with the parents of kids who came to this workshop. Together we made and floated clouds on helium balloons like we do in our show. All the clouds were released in one celebratory moment to the top of the library's atrium, forming a big indoor sky.
- Community feast—PearlDamour hosted a big New Orleans-style dinner in the community center for locals we were working with, and anyone new interested in the project. We gave a slideshow talk about the project. Heritage Club students helped out.
- Local artist roundtable at Frazier Farmstead—PearlDamour hosted a series of roundtables for local artists to discuss what they needed to make their work in Milton-Freewater and how Milton-Freewater could be a more nurturing artistic home. One need was for more consistent artist gatherings in town to build camaraderie and boost morale.

SPRING:
- Creative workshops with high-school and middle-school classes.
- Arts Portal Gallery opening and exhibition—We initiated a collaboration between Jean Ann Mitchell of the Arts Portal Gallery and Jenny Hegdal, the middle-school art teacher. Jenny's students made paintings about their dreams for Milton-Freewater, which were exhibited alongside adult artists' work in the Arts Portal Gallery's spring show.
- School performances at Cinco de Mayo—Shakespeare Walla Walla worked with middle-school students to bring an original, abridged *Romeo and Juliet* set in Milton-Freewater to the festival.

- Dream Booth at Cinco de Mayo Festival—PearlDamour created a "Dream Booth" for the festival, where people could enter a colorful tent with interior walls painted with mountain ranges. Guests were encouraged to write a dream for Milton-Freewater on a cloud, and pin it to the horizon.
- Heritage Club story circle—This family event was an afternoon of story sharing and cultural mapping games. We worked with the Heritage Club throughout the year, training them to lead the event.

SUMMER:

- PearlDamour's *MILTON* performance, Dream Booth, and community cookout—We presented four performances of *MILTON* in the McLoughlin High Auditorium. Excerpts of the completed bilingual version of the show are printed in Appendix A. We hosted a well-attended community cookout on the high-school lawn before our matinee. Our Dream Booth was set up in the lobby of the theater to visit before or after the show.
- Lark in the Park—A locally initiated get-together in a local park—a time for artists to come together and make work outdoors.

FOLLOW UP / THE FUTURE:

In Milton-Freewater, OR, the pop-up art galleries continue. The equipment that the artists were able to purchase with money from a grant we wrote allows them to have live music at all of their openings—and they are considering spoken-word nights in the gallery as well.

MILTON, MA—MILTON REFLECTING

THE NEED:

Milton, MA, is known primarily as a wealthy suburb of Boston. Our conversations here aren't about a town disappearing, but about rapidly changing racial demographics in a town led primarily by the white "old guard." Our local stakeholders are eager for consistent, creative opportunities to have nuanced, ongoing conversations about race.

DEVELOPING THE IDEA:

We'd been visiting Milton, MA for about three years when it came time to produce our show. We'd gotten to know a range of individuals and community groups, so when we sat down with our key partners to discuss a formal collaboration, the ideas came flying. All were related to the changing racial dynamics and legacy of white supremacy in Milton, along with the multiplicity of experience in the town, and the desire to celebrate this multiplicity by facilitating relationships among the town's different ethnic groups.

The planning group began to formulate a program called Milton Reflecting: a full year of creative activities designed to bring Miltonians of all ages together to reflect on and activate the extraordinary diversity of the town. With the town, we applied for and recieved our second NEA Our Town Grant.

Our application was ambitious: art installations in the library, a series of story circles, book discussion groups, children's diversity programming, playwriting workshops in eldercare facilities, the production of our play, and a program called Sacred Conversations (later renamed Courageous Conversations) spearheaded by the Milton Interfaith Clergy Association, designed to be a safe, facilitated space for people to talk about race.

KEY PARTNERS (PEOPLE AND ORGANIZATIONS):

- The Milton Public Library—Library director Will Adamczyk, a white man and early advocate of our project, was our primary civic partner on our NEA Our Town Grant and throughout the project. The library became the home base for Milton Reflecting, hosting installations, activities, and ultimately our play. Milton Reflecting became part of the library's five-year plan to widen and diversify patronage.

- Citizens for a Diverse Milton (CDM)—The founders of CDM were among the first Miltonians we met in town: a group committed to working towards racial parity, especially in the faculty and staff of the school system. One of CDM's founders came to the performance in Milton, NC as an ambassador from Massachusetts, and became a strong advocate for bringing the show to Milton, MA.

- Milton Interfaith Clergy Association (MICA)—MICA is a fantastic group of local church leaders interested in facilitating collegiality and conversations among people of all faiths. We met Reverend Hall Kirkham, a key member of the group, at an early community event, and he immediately saw the kinship between our project and MICA's mission.

- Ron Bell—A community organizer who hosted a local access Milton Reflecting TV show with project updates and interviews with local leaders. Ron, an African American man, worked hard to spread word of the project through the Black community.

- Karen Groce-Horan—We met Karen, a Black woman, as a member of CDM; she quickly became our most devoted community advocate and partner, and an important connector for us.

- Winter Valley, Fuller Village, Unquity House—We worked in many ways with these three eldercare facilities: interviewing residents, giving project talks, and hosting creative writing workshops which led to an Elder Play Festival at Fuller Village and Unquity House.

- Boston Playwrights' Theatre (BPT) —We partnered with Boston Playwrights' Theatre on all activities related to the Elder Play Festival. Graduate student writers held writing workshops and recruited professional local actors to perform in the playfest.

THE EVENTS:
Working with Milton, MA was different from the other Miltons: it was bigger, and radiated an urban, East-coast sensibility. Local partners had a huge capacity to organize, write grants, and use social media to mobilize their communities. These Miltonians were also BUSY, and so they took more convincing than the folks in the smaller Miltons. Did they really have room in their lives for a creative project like ours?

Funding was surprisingly difficult to come by. Known as a "wealthy" town, there was a prevailing perception that Milton didn't need grant money. And competition for grants in Massachusetts is much steeper than it is in say, Eastern Oregon or rural North Carolina. Once our team came together, however, there was fantastic group energy to find the funding. When we recieved our NEA Our Town funding, we launched the following activities as part of Milton Reflecting:

LIBRARY INSTALLATIONS AND COMMUNITY DREAMCATCHER:

The library served as home base for Milton Reflecting. We produced two month-long installations in the library's open gallery space with audio and photos from all five Miltons, along with artifacts and video from our show. We also hung a giant dream catcher created by a local artist in the lobby and invited patrons to hang their dreams for Milton from the dream catcher. The library planned to gather and collate the dream strips, then pass them on to town leaders.

COURAGEOUS CONVERSATIONS:

Karen Groce-Horan worked with her church and MICA to launch Courageous Conversations. She has now established it as a monthly event that travels to churches on all sides of Milton. At meetings, diverse groups of up to 60 people come together to discuss different books or films that open up multiple perspectives on race and the experience of living in this country, and in Milton.

MLK DAY EVENT:

Milton Reflecting was the "keynote speaker" at Milton's MLK Day service at Concord Baptist Church. Katie joined Karen and Ron to set up a conversation activity that happened right in the middle of the service—two-person story-sharings about experiences of inclusion/exclusion and comfort/discomfort, which were then shared with the larger congregation.

ELDER PLAY FEST:

We hosted a special performance at Fuller Village of scenes written for and with elders in town, facilitated by the Boston Playwrights' Theatre playwrights and performed by professional actors. The structure of the performance was based on BPT's long-time school program called New Noises. It worked great, and a small-scale version of the show was reprised at Unquity House as a daytime event for residents who couldn't get to the evening performance.

STORY CIRCLES, BOOK CLUBS, AND DIVERSITY PROGRAMMING:

The library used Milton Reflecting to help develop diversity-focused activities as part of their kids' programming each month. We held a few sessions of a book group led by the library director, discussing books that focused on the diverse histories of Milton, but not enough people showed up so we let that go. We launched the Milton Reflecting year with three story circles, and after that we focused on Courageous Conversations.

MILTON, THE PLAY:

We wrote this draft of the play based on the input of local partners who wanted the performance to address issues of race head on. It took place in a multi-purpose meeting and education room of the library, with chairs on wooden risers in a circle. This was a basement room, so the ceiling was too low for us to hang our plexiglass screens. Instead, we projected ovals of sky on the walls and ceiling. We did evening and weekend shows, as well as morning shows for high school sophomores.

AND THEN / THE FUTURE:

In Milton, MA, the legacy of our project has been starting conversations in various community forums and spaces. Courageous Conversations is now a monthly reading and discussion series hosted by a different church each month. The event cuts across race and class in Milton, regularly hosting a mix of people at each conversation. Our Milton Reflecting community dream catcher still hangs in the library's atrium as a visual reminder of the value of shared visioning.

c: funding strategies

We had no idea how much this project was going to cost when we started—or really what the funding landscape might be for a project like this. As our community engagement work deepened and expanded, especially in Milton-Freewater, OR and Milton, MA, our budgets got bigger and bigger. Here are the ways we funded the project throughout its life span:

MULTI ARTS PRODUCTION FUND (MAP):
- Launched the project by paying for our first round of site visits. We first thought the MAP grant could cover the entire *MILTON* project but realized quickly it wouldn't even cover one of the Miltons—in part because we wanted to focus significant time and energy on each town, which required a lot of travel and housing; in part because we wanted to produce a full show, which required significant design elements.
- MAP also gave us sessions with a project consultant who helped us decide to put all our resources into completing one complete iteration of the project in Milton, NC, which could then serve as a model for the others and give us work samples that could help us raise more money.
- MAP funding allowed us to buy our equipment so we had a self-contained touring kit.

NEW YORK STATE COUNCIL ON THE ARTS (NYSCA):
Supported New York workshops, development sessions, public showings, and the publication of this book.

CROWDFUNDING:
This was, for us, a massive fundraising effort—$20,000. Most of the money we raised went towards making the project happen in Milton, NC. It also supported the development of our *MILTON* website, and raised awareness about the project.

DORIS DUKE PERFORMING ARTIST AWARD:
Awarded to Lisa. This comes with $25,000 in audience development funds, and Lisa committed $12,500 to *MILTON* and $12,500 to future PearlDamour projects.

WORKING FOR FREE:

During the initial phase and the Milton, NC prep, both of us agreed to work for no salary (only a per diem while traveling), since Lisa had the Doris Duke and Katie had a grad school fellowship.

NETWORK OF ENSEMBLE THEATERS TRAVEL GRANT:

Brought us to Durham, NC to work with a local company. From there it was short drive to get to Milton, NC.

LOCAL AND REGIONAL GRANTS:

In all three Miltons we worked with local partners to secure regional grants. These grants rarely went specifically to our show, but rather supported and catalyzed locally driven projects or enabled our partner organizations to purchase needed equipment or update old electrical systems in our performance venues.

- **NC:** *Danville Regional Foundation (formerly Dan River Foundation)*
- **OR:** *Autzen Foundation, Oregon Arts Commission, Collins Foundation*
- **MA:** *Celebrate Milton, Copeland Family Foundation, Milton Junior Women's Club*

NEA OUR TOWN GRANTS:

After Milton, NC we were awarded Our Town Grants for both Milton-Freewater, OR and Milton, MA. These 1:1 matching grants spurred the projects to grow much bigger, and also incited vigorous work to find local and regional funding.

WORKSHOP RESIDENCIES:

The project was made possible in large part by workshop residencies at Brown University, where we developed the script and staging/scenic strategies, and Berkeley Rep Ground Floor, where we pulled together the final draft of the script and presented a rehearsal reading of the show with music. A 2016-2017 residency teaching students how to make community-based works at the University of Washington was also helpful—getting us to the Milton-Freewater region regularly and reducing travel costs. UW also provided rehearsal space as we prepped for our Milton-Freewater show.

d: music

Score

Places (a driving tour)

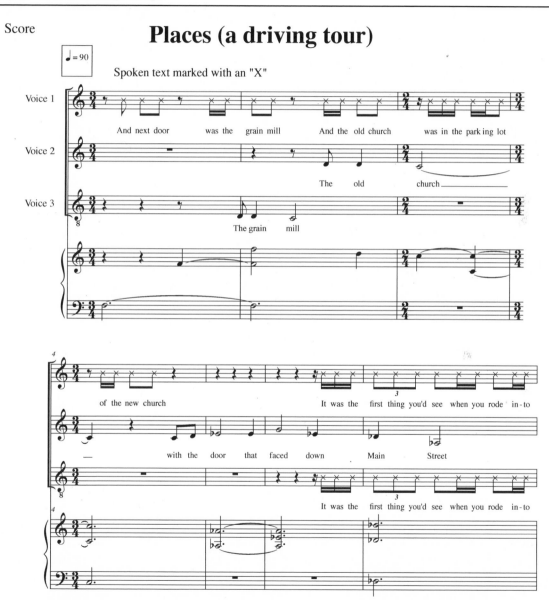

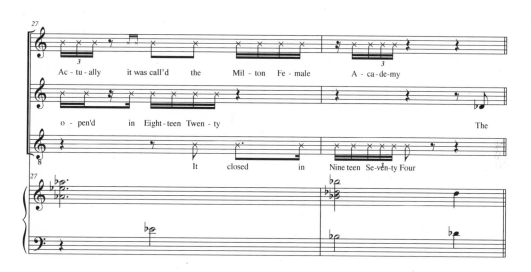

Ac - tu - ally it was call'd the Mil - ton Fe - male A - ca - de-my

o - pen'd in Eight-teen Twen - ty The

It closed in Nine teen Se-ven-ty Four

where we use'd to dance the Ca-jun Waltz. the foot - ball field for the

dance hall _____ Mil-ton Col lege the buildings are still there

the col - lege _____ mmm it went

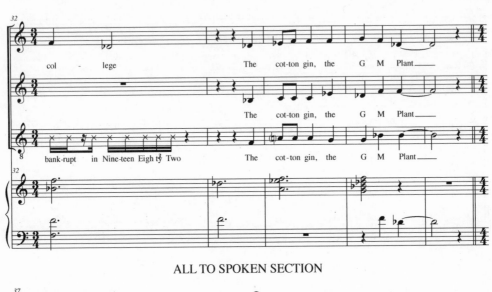

ALL TO SPOKEN SECTION

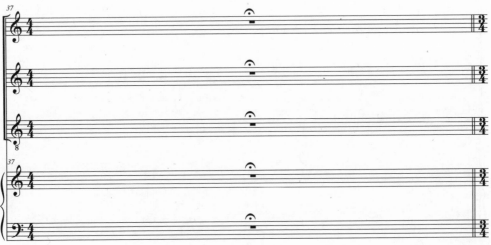

Sub-di-vi-sion mid-dle school Farm-land

Farm-land called Su-gar Lake Pond the best in La-fa yette Pa rish a

Farm - land Farm - land

leased for hor-ses Farm-land Still farm-land

block of hou-ses Farm-land Still arm-land

Farm-land Farm-land Still farm-land

but the guy who farms it   is   not from a - round____   here.

Objects

Spoken text marked with an "X"

At the end of your in-ter-view   some-one gives you   a t-shirt   from their

some-times   a   jar   of   fig   preserves   a t-shirt   from their

Cath-lic Church   there is a   book a-bout the Dan   Ri-ver

Bi-ker Club   And   some-times   you walk in-to a   conven-tion cen-ter   and   find a

bowl-ing al-ley   And   then   and a-   gain

There is a stage

"We also saw those in a frame
on the wall of the pecan
farmer's house in Louisiana"

in a wheel chair deck'd out with party lights and a sound system

on the front lawn

On the front lawn

Visibility is Low

Vi si bil-i-ty   is   low to day

I - can bare-ly see my haaa - nd

We call this low vi si - bil - i -ty____

When you can see as far as   Hoton's

Pond   that   means____ vi si - bil -i-ty____ is bet - ter____

This is a ve - ry typ-i-cal   fog

Clo - uds: see them drift - ing   o - ver - the sum-mit?

There they are right

e: miltonians we met

LOUISIANA:

Henrietta Schilling, Tia Trahan, Joyce Broussard, Beverly and Caroll Spell, Doug and Sue Duhon, Wilma B. Landry, George "Wa Wee" Broussard, Nola Broussard, Rennie Broussard, Maude Picard, Janell and Junor, Caroll Duhon, Janel Viator, Amber Guidroz, Lisa Broussard, Paula and John Landry, Emily Landry, Ed and Jeannette Hebert, Frankie Landry, Barb, Elaine Lareade-Bourque, Mary Jane and Liz, Bobby and Enola Broussard, Kathy Mulloy, Deacon Soley, Mae, Pris Hebert, Janice Simon

MASSACHUSETTS:

Mark Conrad, John Cronin and Maritta Cronin, Mallory Diggs, Rita Feeney, Myrtle Flight, Myrna Friedman, Mary Gormley, Kristen Grassel Schmidt, Phil Hennesey, Patricia Hoy Reilly, Scott Huntoon, Brian Kelley, Marie Klaus, Sally Lawler, Don McCasland, Deborah Milbauer, Andy Ortiz, Eleanor Tobias, Peggy Walsh, Amy Gale, Bill Deschenes, Claudia Greene, Chris Navin, Cynthia Guise, Peggy Albers Aubin, Pat Latimore, Will Adamczyk, Pat Desmond, Carline Desiré, Guy Apollon, Becky Padera, Dennis Slaughter, Tom Pilla, Molly Mullen and Dad, Liz O'Rourke-Harris, Jessica Sueiro, Tiffany Kearney, Renee Chiu, Amory Files, James Lê, Hall Kirkham, Joyce Caggiano, Javana Samuels, Brian Doherty, Karen Groce-Horan, Christina Mines, Jennifer Manak, Tanya Frank, Emily Martin, David Burnes, Tom Hurley, Katie Conlon, Jeff Stone, Beth Olson, Isabelle from Fuller Village, Marilyn Cheney, Nancy Selig, Lisa Ramsay, Bob Wolff, Greg Gordon, Penny Knight, Barbara Piper, Dawn Duncan, Ron Bell, Rick Penderhughes, Sue Hoy, Barbara Wright, Jaymes Sanchez, Nancy Warn, Ricky Cintron, Catherine Troutman, Ginny Kime, Rachel Pettengill-Rasure, Elizabeth Thomas, Kathryn Johnson, Becky Warner, Teresa Desmond, Audeline Eugene, Blossom Glassman, Agnes Ortiz, Conley Hughes, Shelly Davis, Franc Graham, Joan Moynagh, Jean Hlady

NORTH CAROLINA:

Cleota Jeffries, Anne Haley, Michael Bryant, Mayor Harriet Brandon, Hosanna and Kevin Blanchard, Shirley Cadmus, Shirley and Ronnie Wilson, Cathia and Elmer Stewart, Joetta Mabe, Sally Wallace, John G. Wallace, Jr., Larry Jeffries, Jean Scott, Gwen McGuire, Rev. John Upton, Marian Thomas, Rev. Clyde Everett, Rev. Angel Lea and Donald Lea, Patsy and Oliver at the Tire and Grill, Anne Poole, Mary Beth Howe, Clay and Staten Angle, Jackson McSherry, Ann Scott, Joe and Sue Graves, Daily Slade, Nancy Hughes, Lynn Nash, Katherine McGee, Jim Upchurch, Moe Hooper, Dotti, Josh Aldridge, Mike Behler, Mary Beth, Jack Williams, Twinkle Graves, Herman and Julia Joubert, Elizabeth and Bo Pressley, J.R. Whitt, Sherri Meyers-Keatts, Julie and Craig at the Tap and Dye, Pastor Kelvin Royster, Jeff Henderson, Clint Briggs, Dustin Chism, Taco and Rhona Smith, David Porterfield, Mark Cornelius, John Greene, Luke Lunsford, Martin Owen, Jason Thompson, H. Lee Fowlkes Jr., Carolyn Dixson, Stephen Harris, Walter Woickowsfski, Diane Kendrick, Jackie Jeffries, Jean Vernon, Druscilla McCain

OREGON:
Diane Biggs, Tori Banek, Bob "Library Bob" Jones, John "Santa" Perkins, Jan Sample, Alina Launchbaugh, Esmerelda Perez, Merton Heidenrich, Kelly Smith, Julie Culjak, Geri Honn, Linda Hall, Norm Saager, Sam Hubbard, Clive Kaiser, Filrobert Chavez, Cuco, Father Charles, Mike Watkins, Sharame Marlatt, Gerry Seagreave, Norma Kerby, Gerry Reese, Lan Wong, Mayor Lewis Key, Daynis Garcia, Joceline Luis, Grasiela Ramos, Clariluel, Mayra Osorio, Ron Saager, Diedre Nyburg, Joe and Lauren (the shoe technicians at Saager's Shoes), Alfonso Matinez, Ana Bueno-Salazar, Betty Wood, Blanche Mason, Brad Humbert, Brandon Hallsted, Brenda Thomas, Broderick Graves, Carlos Vargas- Salgado, Carol Burks, Celeste Kemmerer, Charlotte Trumbull, Cheryl York, Chris Chesteru, Chuck Frates, Judy Witherrite, Curtis Steele, Daynis Garcia, Eduardo Corona, Elda Jimenez, Elvira Martinez, Erin Wells, Felex Pereyda, Sandra Pereyda, Fermin Mendoza, Fran Walker, Frank Jienez, Gina Hartheim, Isabel and Junior Flores, Jean Ann Mitchell, Jennifer Hilton, Jennifer Beckmeyer, Jenn Zerba, Jenny Hegdal, Johnny Robles, Jose Garcia, Juan Fuentes, Lan Wong, Lilli Schmidt, Nelsa Boisjolie, Norma Kerby, Ramone Esparza, Randy Grant, Rob Clark, Ron Williams, Shane Abell, Sharame Marlatt, Taylor Johnson, Teresa Dutcher, Tracey Rambo, Victor Corona, Sandy Snook, Eva Saldaña, the students of the Mac Hi Heritage Club, Melissa Cunnington and her drama students

WISCONSIN:
Toni and Todd Williams and Cody of Varsity Lanes, Kelly and Scott Richardson, Lisa Brooks, Brett Frazier, David the Director of The Gathering Place, Duke and Annette Siegfried, John Shultz, Ondra Williams, Phyllis Siverly, Dawn and Roger Jensen, Brenda Bender, Leann Wasemiller, Judy Sheeley,

Lois Harris, James Deblizen, AL Astin, Betty Ronde, Sandy Metcalf, Jim and Linda Lyke, Connor Goggans, Andy Sanchez, Pam, Tim Scheiger, Betty Hoag, Abib Zonouzi, Dona and Brad Dutcher, Connie Bier, Chef David, Frankie Giffone, Cori from the Milton House, Rob Johnson, Joshua Weiss and his students at MECAS, Ashlee Kunkel, the Cruzans

. . . and so many others. Our deepest thanks to everyone we met in our travels through the Miltons, and apologies to those whose names we've left out—you're in our minds and hearts!

bios

PearlDamour is the Obie-Award winning collaborative team of Katie Pearl and Lisa D'Amour. For over 20 years, PearlDamour has pushed the boundaries of theatrical experience both inside and outside traditional theater spaces, devising a body of work crafted through long-form collaborations with artists from other fields. Collaborators include visual artists Krista Kelley Walsh, Charles Goldman, and Shawn Hall; set designer Mimi Lien; video artist Jim Findlay; choreographer Emily Johnson; composers Brendan Connelly, Sxip Shirey, Joel Pickard, and Tom McDermott; director/performer Kathy Randels; and community engagement expert Ashley Sparks. PearlDamour's work includes *How to Build a Forest*, a durational performance installation in which a simulated forest is assembled and disassembled on an empty stage over eight hours, and *Lost in the Meadow*, created for the 46-acre Meadow Garden at Longwood Botanical Gardens outside Philadelphia. PearlDamour's work has been commissioned and presented by PS122, The Kitchen, the Whitney Museum of Art, People's Light and Theatre, and the American Repertory Theater/Harvard Center for the Environment. Other presenters include the Walker Arts Center, HERE Arts Center, the Fusebox Festival, Magdalena Festival, Ko Festival, ArtSpot Productions and many universities throughout the U.S. PearlDamour has received project support from the NEA, Creative Capital, MAP Fund, and NYSCA, among others. They were honored with the Lee Reynolds Award in 2011 for *How to Build a Forest*, and with an Obie Award in 2003 for *Nita and Zita*. pearldamour.com

Brendan Connelly is a composer and sound designer, and has worked with PearlDamour, Jim Findlay, Suzan-Lori Parks, Anne Kauffmann, Jody McAuliffe, David Levine, Tom Murrin, Ian Belton and many others. He co-founded the Obie-winning Two-headed Calf (with Brooke O'Harra) and has composed music for all of its productions. His music has been performed by Yarn/Wire, SEM Ensemble, Timetable Percussion, Wet Ink Ensemble and many others. He is an alum of the NEZ/TCG program and teaches electronic music at Tulane University.

Jim Findlay works across boundaries as a theater artist, visual artist, and filmmaker. His work includes his original performances "Vine of the Dead" (2015), "Dream of the Red Chamber" (2014), "Botanica" (2012) and the direction and design of David Lang's "Whisper Opera" (2014). He is a founding member of the Collapsable Giraffe and, in partnership with Radiohole, founded the Collapsable Hole, a multi-disciplinary artist-led performance venue in Manhattan's West Village. His work has been seen at Lincoln Center, Carnegie Hall, BAM, Arena Stage, A.R.T. and over 50 cities internationally.

Ashley Sparks is a freelance southern theatre-maker, engagement strategist, and facilitator. She has worked across the U.S. in New Orleans, Wilmington, Stuarts Draft, Milton, Baltimore, and Los Angeles, with such companies as Cornerstone Theater Company, ArtSpot Productions, and PearlDamour. As a director her work is focused on creating site-specific devised work and participatory events that may involve line dancing, gospel singing, or playing with remote-control cars. As an engagement strategist she coaches artists and organizations to deepen the connection art can have with specific audiences. As a curator and producer Ashley leads national convenings for the Network for Energy, Water, and Health in Affordable Buildings. She was the Project Director for the Network of Ensemble Theaters MicroFest USA event series. She is a Princess Grace Honoree and a Blade of Grass Fellow for *Good Old Boys*. She holds an MFA in Directing and Public Dialogue from Virginia Tech University.

Thank you to **Eleanor Savage** for working with us to develop the Sky Over Milton website.

This book is dedicated to the memory of **Nola and George Broussard** of Milton, NC. Thank you for lending your voices to our play.

53rd state

Book design + layout: Tyler Crumrine
Cover design: Jonathan Crimmins
Cover image: *Atlas coalestis* by John Flamsteed (1646-1719)

53rd State Press publishes lucid, challenging, and lively new writing for performance. Our catalog includes new plays as well as scores and notations for interdisciplinary performance, graphic adaptations, and essays on theater and dance.

53rd State Press was founded in 2007 by Karinne Keithley in response to the bounty of new writing in the downtown New York community that was not available except in the occasional reading or short-lived performance. In 2010, Antje Oegel joined her as a co-editor. In 2017, Kate Kremer took over the leadership of the volunteer editorial collective: Laurel Atwell, Tymberly Canale, and Anne Cecelia DeMelo.

For more information or to order books, please visit 53rdstatepress.org.

53rd State Press books are available to the trade through TCG (Theater Communications Group) and are distributed by Consortium: https://cbsd.com.

MILTON is made possible by the New York State Council on the Arts with the support of Governor Andrew M. Cuomo and the New York State Legislature.

also from 53rd state press

FORTHCOMING